College Composition
MODULAR

CLEP* Test Study Guide

> All rights reserved. This Study Guide, Book and Flashcards are protected under the US Copyright Law. No part of this book or study guide or flashcards may be reproduced, distributed or stored in a retrieval system, or transmitted in any form or by any means, electronic, mechanical, photocopying, recording, or otherwise, without the prior written permission of the publisher Breely Crush Publishing, LLC.

© 2020 Breely Crush Publishing, LLC

*CLEP is a registered trademark of the College Entrance Examination Board which does not endorse this book.

971010420143

Copyright ©2003 - 2020, Breely Crush Publishing, LLC.

All rights reserved.

This Study Guide, Book and Flashcards are protected under the US Copyright Law. No part of this publication may be reproduced, distributed or stored in a retrieval system, or transmitted in any form or by any means, electronic, mechanical, photocopying, recording, or otherwise, without the prior written permission of the publisher Breely Crush Publishing, LLC.

Published by Breely Crush Publishing, LLC
10808 River Front Parkway
South Jordan, UT 84095
www.breelycrushpublishing.com

ISBN-10: 1-61433-631-8
ISBN-13: 978-1-61433-631-0

Printed and bound in the United States of America.

*CLEP is a registered trademark of the College Entrance Examination Board which does not endorse this book.

Table of Contents

About the CLEP College Composition Modular Examination 1
    Definitions/Explanations of Types of Questions 1
    Skills Tested 1
Other Study Materials 2
Practice Test Questions 3
    Identifying Sentence Errors 3
    Pronouns 3
Agreement of Subject and Verb 5
Word Choices, Diction, and Idioms 6
Parallelism 7
Dangling and Misplaced Modifiers 8
Verb Forms 9
Sentence Problems 10
Improving Sentences 11
Restructuring Sentences 13
Revising Work in Progress 15
Analyzing Sentences 21
Essay Writing 25
Strategy for Writing the Entire Essay 26
    Strategy for Writing Each Paragraph 27
5 x 5 Paragraph Essay 28
Practice Essay Topics 28
Formats and Documentation 29
Reference Skills 33
Use of Reference Books 34
Footnotes and Endnotes 34
Word Choice and Idiom Review 37
    Commonly Misused Words 37
    Commonly Misused Idiomatic Prepositional Phrases 38
Exam Tips 39
Study Guide Answer Key 40
    Identifying Sentence Errors 40
Additional Practice Test 43
    I. Punctuation 43
    II. Combined Sentences 44
    III. Possessives 45
    IV. Subordination and Coordination 47
    V. Identifying Sentence Errors 48
    VI. Improving Sentences 49

*VII. Following is a Draft of a Student Composition with the
    Sentences Numbered for Reference* *51*
*VIII. Following is a Paragraph From the Draft of a Student
    Composition with the Sentences Numbered for Reference* *53*
IX. Word Choice and Idiom *55*
X. Verb Forms *56*

Answer Key *58*
Test-Taking Strategies *59*
What Your Score Means *59*
Test Preparation *60*
Legal Note *60*

 About the CLEP College Composition Modular Examination

Which version are you taking? Your school can choose to use their own essay or the CLEP essay. If your school chooses to use the essays from CLEP, you will have to write two essays in 70 minutes. This is in addition to the multiple choice section which includes 90 questions to be answered in 90 minutes.

DEFINITIONS/EXPLANATIONS OF TYPES OF QUESTIONS

Each of the following types of test questions will be covered in this study guide. Each type will have questions and contain explanations and instructions useful for answering the questions.

Identifying Sentence Errors: Identify wording that goes against the standard conventions of written English.
Improving Sentences: Select the phrase, clause, or sentence that best expresses the intended meaning.
Restructuring Sentences: Choose the phrase, among five options, which will change emphasis or improve clarity in the sentence.
Revising Work in Progress: Identify ways to improve a rough draft of an essay.
Analyzing Writing: Answer questions about each passage's content and organization and each author's strategies.

SKILLS TESTED

CLEP examination questions are based on the following skills:

Sentences:

- Sentence boundaries
- Active/passive voice
- Agreement (subject/verb, pronoun/antecedent)
- Sentence completeness and variety
- Idiom and diction
- Economy and clarity of expression
- Syntax: parallelism, coordination, subordination, dangling modifiers

Context:

- Thesis, or main idea
- Organization of a paragraph or essay
- Style, tone, language, or argument's purpose
- Logic of argument (inductive/deductive reasoning)
- Point of view and rhetorical emphasis
- Sufficient details and relevant evidence
- Sentence joining and variety (parallelism, coordination, subordination, modification)
- Coherence and sustaining appropriate tense

Other Study Materials

It is always a good idea to have a few other resources available, books and websites, as you study for the CLEP College Composition Modular Examination. The following are some suggestions.

http://english-zone.com/ This site covers grammar, paragraph writing, and tips for studying.
http://grammar.ccc.commnet.edu/grammar/ This site is a good resource for reviewing grammar at the sentence level and paragraph level. If you are taking the essay version of the CLEP, it also has good advice for writing.
http://www.studygs.net/ This is a well-rounded site with information on writing essays

Good, Edward C. A Grammar Book For You and I (Oops, Me) All the Grammar You Need to Succeed in Life. Capital Books Inc., 2002
Shertzer, Margaret D. The Elements of Grammar. New York: Macmillan General Reference, 1996
Strunk Jr., William and White, E.B. The Elements of Style. New York: Macmillan Publishing Company, 1979

 # Practice Test Questions

IDENTIFYING SENTENCE ERRORS

> **Note:** For purposes of reviewing the different types of grammatical error, the practice questions for Identifying Sentence Errors will be organized separately in this study guide. They are not separated by error on the CLEP examination.

The categories are: pronouns; agreement of subject and verb; word choices, diction, and idioms; parallelism; dangling and misplaced modifiers; and verb forms.

Directions: The following questions will test your knowledge of grammar, usage, diction (choice of words), and idiom. Each item has four underlined elements with a corresponding letter (A), (B), (C), and (D). Each item also has a possible selection choice of letter (E) "no error." If you find an error, select the one underlined part that has to change to make the sentence correct.

PRONOUNS

Pronouns agree with the noun they represent (antecedent) in gender and number.

Nominative case (I, you, she, he, we, you, they)
Objective case (me, you, her, him, us, them)
Possessive case (my, mine, your, yours, his, her, hers, its, our, ours, their, theirs)
Compound personal pronouns (myself, yourself, himself, herself, itself, ourselves, yourselves, themselves)
Relative Pronouns (who, that, which, what) Pay special attention to *who*, which changes its form to indicate case (who, whose, whom, whoever, whomever)
Interrogative Pronouns (who, which, what)
Indefinite Pronouns (all, any, both, each, either, everybody, none, one, several, some, someone)

1. Mrs. Orzo is a wonderful <u>woman whom always</u> has a positive <u>attitude and a</u>
                                        A   B
   <u>warm</u> smile <u>even when</u> there is nothing to <u>smile about</u>. <u>No error</u>.
     C   D   E

2. <u>The dormitory room was</u> the size of a closet, <u>which I knew</u> would mean
            A   B
   trouble for <u>Nancy and I</u> in terms of <u>our future</u> friendship. <u>No error</u>.
                C   D   E

3. After telling <u>my father</u> of the airline reservations <u>I had made</u>, <u>he disapproved</u>
                A   B   C
   <u>of me</u> traveling; <u>he said it was</u> too far. <u>No error</u>.
     D   E

4. Emily Bronte, <u>who's writing</u> is said to be the best among <u>her sisters</u>,
                  A   B
   <u>has only written</u> and published *Wuthering Heights* and yet <u>it takes its place</u>
      C   D
   alongside the masterpieces of English literature. <u>No error</u>.
                                           E

5. Upton Sinclair gained fame and fortune <u>with his novel</u> *The Jungle* and with
                                           A
   <u>it's uncovering of</u> the dirty conditions in <u>the Chicago meatpacking industry</u> that
        B   C
   led to the <u>implementation of</u> the Pure Food and Drug Act in 1906. <u>No error</u>.
                D   E

6. After reading the book <u>that he wrote</u>, <u>I thought to myself</u> what a great guy he
                              A   B
   was for crediting <u>whomever gave him</u> the inspiration <u>he needed</u> to strive for a
                          C   D
   better life. <u>No error</u>.
                E

7. After using the techniques <u>Brigitte learned</u> in acting class, <u>she was</u> able to relax
                             A   B
   <u>herself</u> while taking <u>the exam</u>. <u>No error</u>.
     C   D   E

8. When <u>Elizabeth tells everyone</u> that <u>she is</u> really happy, it is because <u>she is</u> trying
                  A   B   C
   to convince <u>herself</u>. <u>No error</u>.
            D   E

 # Agreement of Subject and Verb

Agreement of subject and verb means they are in the same singular or plural form. For more information and a short quiz, take a look at this site:
http://grammar.ccc.commnet.edu/grammar/

1. Rita and <u>Philip is</u> going <u>to take</u> the advanced <u>Shakespeare course</u> in order <u>to earn</u>
                 A   B   C   D
   extra credit. <u>No error</u>.
                 E

2. <u>A newspaper</u> for instance <u>may look</u> innocent enough, but <u>propaganda can be</u>
       A   B   C
   created just by the words <u>they choose</u>. <u>No error</u>.
                           D   E

3. <u>The article claims that</u> the <u>media are</u> responsible <u>for the negative</u> influences <u>it has</u>
             A   B   C   D
   on children. <u>No error</u>.
               E

4. <u>It was</u> an unfortunate situation when <u>neither</u> the <u>lifeguard nor</u> the <u>doctors was</u>
     A   B   C   D
   <u>able</u> to revive the victim. <u>No error</u>.
                             E

5. <u>The recipe</u> asks for <u>one cup of sugar, but</u> either one cup of honey <u>or two cups of</u>
       A   B   C
   applesauce <u>are good substitutes</u>. <u>No error</u>.
                D   E

Word Choices, Diction, and Idioms

Word choices are sometimes mistaken for other words that sound the same, but are spelled differently and have different meanings or are assumed to have the same meaning, but do not. *See page 25 for a list of some types of commonly misused words.*

Diction errors are incorrect word choices. *Idiom* errors are expressions that are not always clear from the meaning of words (kick the bucket).

1. <u>My science project</u>, <u>which won second place</u>, determined <u>the affects</u> of sunlight
         A   B   C
   <u>deprivation in people</u>. <u>No error</u>.
         D   E

2. I <u>would of</u> gladly <u>taken Isabelle to the concert</u> yesterday if she <u>wasn't so</u>
       A   B   C
   demanding when <u>she asked me</u>. <u>No error</u>.
                           D   E

3. <u>I am amazed</u> that <u>my five-year-old</u> sister knows the <u>capitol cities</u> of <u>fifteen states</u>.
         A   B   C   D
   <u>No error</u>.
     E

4. My day <u>was going good</u> until <u>I heard the news</u> about <u>our term papers</u> being
                  A   B   C
   <u>due on Monday</u>. <u>No error</u>.
       D   E

5. <u>The neurologist said</u> there is a <u>definite relationship</u> between the <u>paint fumes</u> and
         A   B   C
   <u>your headache</u>. <u>No error</u>.
       D   E

6. <u>Between those seven colors</u>, the <u>customer chose</u> the <u>green and blue ones</u> to
            A   B   C
   <u>decorate</u> her living room. <u>No error</u>.
      D   E

 Parallelism

In order for a sentence with a list of two or more items to be parallel, it has to have the same grammatical structure. You can usually spot parallel construction errors because they sound awkward. For more information and a quiz on parallelism, look at these sites:
http://webster.commnet.edu/grammar/parallelism.htm
http://webster.commnet.edu/grammar/quizzes/niu/niu10.htm

EXAMPLE:

   (parallel) She said <u>that she would go to</u> the play, <u>that her husband would go to</u> the doctor, and <u>that her daughter would go to</u> school.

   (not parallel) She said that she would go to the play, her husband should go to the doctor, and her daughter would be at school.

Directions: Choose the underlined phrase that is a parallel construction error.

1. I thought it <u>couldn't be done</u>, but on her lunch break <u>she washed her cat</u>, <u>had her car fixed</u>, and <u>cleaned her house</u>. <u>No error</u>.
             A   B   C   D   E

2. It <u>would be</u> more reasonable to <u>inspect the plumbing</u>, <u>inspect the roof</u>, and <u>inspect the electrical system</u> today. <u>No error</u>.
   A   B   C   D   E

3. <u>Our beautiful</u> sun <u>rises in the east</u>, is <u>most damaging to us at noon</u>, and <u>sets in the west</u>. <u>No error</u>.
   A   B   C   D   E

4. In order to have a healthy lifestyle one must <u>eat right</u>, <u>exercise enough</u>, and <u>never go on crash diets</u>. <u>No error</u>.
   A   B   C   D

5. Cancer can arise from different external causes such as <u>tobacco smoke</u>, <u>industrial chemicals</u>, <u>X-rays</u>, and <u>perhaps even some types of viruses</u>. <u>No error</u>.
   A   B   C   D   E

 Dangling and Misplaced Modifiers

Modifiers describe words. Sometimes the modifiers are misplaced, resulting in an unclear or comical meaning. A *dangling modifier* does not relate to any other word in its sentence. A *misplaced modifier* relates to the wrong element in its sentence.
Directions: Choose the underlined phrase that cannot modify a word or element.

EXAMPLE:

I. He rode his bike to get to the <u>park in the alley</u>.
It should read: He rode his bike in the alley to get to the park.
<u>park in the alley</u> is the phrase that is unclear.

1. <u>When making</u> the <u>salad at</u> the <u>cooking class</u>, <u>everything was clean</u>. <u>No error</u>.
      A   B   C   D   E

2. <u>After cooling,</u> <u>the chocolate</u> should <u>be poured</u> over <u>the cake</u>. <u>No error</u>.
    A   B   C   D   E

3. <u>I will not give her</u> a <u>good tip</u> since <u>she took</u> my order <u>with a laugh</u>. <u>No error</u>.
      A   B   C   D   E

4. <u>We baked</u> red and <u>green apples</u> at <u>my aunt's</u> house <u>that we picked yesterday</u>.
     A   B   C   D
<u>No error</u>.
  E

5. <u>The sophisticated model</u> was <u>six feet tall</u> with <u>shiny brown</u> hair <u>weighing 120</u>
         A   B   C   D
<u>pounds</u>. <u>No error</u>.
       E

 Verb Forms

A verb tells what the subject does or what is done to it. The verb is an action, mode of being, occurrence, or condition, and should agree with its subject in person and number. *Find out more at:* http://www.grammarstation.com/KnowyourVerb.html

(Forms of the "verb play")
base form	I play
-s form	he/she/it plays
past tense	I played
past participle	I have played
present participle	I am playing

1. College freshmen <u>will become</u> familiar with the campus and <u>become use</u> to <u>their</u>
                            A   B   C
   class schedule <u>within a few weeks</u>. <u>No error</u>.
                           D   E

2. Laura <u>had fell</u> after <u>she jumped</u> over <u>a hurdle</u> in <u>last week's</u> race. <u>No error</u>.
           A   B   C   D   E

3. Sylvia and Livy <u>don't have</u> any more money because <u>the books</u> that they <u>had took</u>
                       A   B   C
   back to the library <u>were damaged</u>. <u>No error</u>.
                       D   E

4. Beverly <u>would not speak</u> to me <u>after she found</u> out I <u>had drank</u> the rest of her
                  A   B   C
   expensive iced tea without <u>asking her for permission</u>. <u>No error</u>.
                            D   E

5. Jill <u>was surprised</u> to find that in her <u>professional working environment</u>, she
         A   B
   <u>had encounter</u> bullies <u>who verbally</u> abused their co-workers. <u>No error</u>.
      C   D   E

 Sentence Problems

A *fragment* is an incomplete sentence that is punctuated as if it were complete. A *comma splice* contains a comma between two independent clauses. A *run-on sentence* contains two independent clauses that are not separated by a conjunction or proper punctuation.

Directions: The following questions will test your knowledge of fragments, comma splices, and run-on sentences. Choose the answer from the revised phrase in (A), (B), (C), (D), or (E).

1) We watched the waves roll toward us, and the sun slowly disappeared from the horizon.

    A) us, when the sun
    B) us, then the sun
    C) us, as the sun
    D) as the sun
    E) us, and had watched as the sun

2) Paul Revere, the son of a Huguenot silversmith a well-known silversmith.

    A) silversmith, was also
    B) silversmith, is
    C) silversmith; was
    D) Paul Revere;
    E) silversmith; a

3) Letters that are handwritten by Abraham Lincoln are widely collected, they are historic and valuable.

    A) collected;
    B) collected, but
    C) collected; historic and valuable.
    D) collected are
    E) collected; which

4) The graduation ceremony complete with music along with teary-eyed parents.

   A) music as well as teary
   B) music was along
   C) music and along
   D) ceremony was completed
   E) ceremony was complete

5) Nepotism is prevalent at that company, all five of the president's spoiled children work there.

   A) company and all
   B) company, which
   C) company; with all five of the president's annoying children working there.
   D) company;
   E) company, the president's spoiled children work there.

Improving Sentences

Directions: The following questions will test your ability to spot the problem in the structure of a sentence. Each sentence item has one underlined element. Choose the appropriate letter choice among (A), (B), (C), (D), or (E) that creates the most effective sentence. Letter choice (A) is the exact underlined element, which you would choose if you think the original sentence is the best. (Think clear and concise).

1) The intuition and strange feelings Nan experiences throughout the novel are <u>not able to be controlled just as falling in love isn't either</u>.

   A) not able to be controlled just as falling in love isn't either.
   B) uncontrollable just as is falling in love.
   C) things she can't control or falling in love.
   D) uncontrollable just as falling in love isn't either.
   E) something she has no control over just as isn't falling in love.

2) <u>When one reads one has to not only take in the author's intent, but always try to think of new things to see besides what the author is saying</u>.

   A) When one reads one has to not only take in the author's intent, but always try to think of new things to see besides what the author is saying.
   B) When one reads, one not only has to consider the author's intent, but also try to think of new ideas besides what the author has in mind.
   C) When reading, one has to realize the author's intent while thinking of new ideas beyond that intent.
   D) As one reads, it is important for them to consider many view points other than just the author's.
   E) Reading requires interpretation of the material in a way that not only recognizes the author's intent, but of new things to see besides what the author is saying.

3) The growing feminist movement brought more women's literature out in the open; <u>however, at the time, university curricula have of course not reflected that movement</u>.

   A) The growing feminist movement brought more women's literature out in the open; however, at the time, university curricula have of course not reflected that movement.
   B) however, university curricula did not reflect that movement.
   C) however, at the time, the universities completely ignored it.
   D) however university curricula were not of course interested in it.
   E) however, at the time, university curricula have of course not been accepting.

4) <u>When a person who experiences more of the active part of learning</u>, there is a greater chance of remembering the information that is being taught.

   A) When a person who experiences more of the active part of learning,
   B) When learning activity is active,
   C) When a person has experienced,
   D) When a person experiences the active part of learning,
   E) When learning is actively done,

5) Despite many hardships throughout author Lucy M. Montgomery's life, <u>she enabled herself to continue writing while to show a happier side of herself</u> in her novels and short stories.

   A) she enabled herself to continue writing while showing a happier side of herself
   B) she enabled herself to continue writing to show a happier side of herself
   C) she continued to write, and show the happier side of herself
   D) she continued writing while a happier side of herself emerged
   E) she continued writing and showing a happier side of herself

Restructuring Sentences

Directions: The following questions will test your ability to restructure a sentence according to given directions. Each item will have one sentence and a set of directions that will require you to change either part or all of the original sentence. Deleting or adding certain words may be necessary in order to construct a clear and concise revised sentence. Choose the correct revision from (A), (B), (C), (D), or (E).

EXAMPLE:

I. **(Sentence)** Should lightning ever cease to exist, plant life would not exist because it needs the nitrogen that lightning produces.

(Directions) Begin with <u>Plant life could not exist.</u>
   A) unless lightning were to happen
   B) if it were not for lightning
   C) without lightning
   D) without
   E) unless

*The answer is (D) without. Therefore, the restructured sentence would read: Plant life could not exist without the nitrogen that lightning produces. The new sentence is clear and omits the repetitive words "exist" and "lightning" while not deviating from the meaning of the original sentence.

1) Deciding to lose her extra weight, Paula joined a health club near her house.

   Change Deciding to Paula decided.

   A) and decided to join
   B) and was joining
   C) and joined
   D) and had joined
   E) and then so she joined

2) When he walks down the hall you know he's coming because the change in his pocket jingles.

   Start with You knew he was coming.

   A) because the change in his pocket jingled when he was walking down the hall.
   B) down the hall because the change in his pocket jingles.
   C) because the change in his pocket had been jingling walking down the hall.
   D) as he was walking down the hall because the change in his pocket jingles.
   E) as he walked down the hall because the change in his pocket were jingling.

3) Corporate America spends billions of dollars in order to create effective propaganda that attempts to control our thoughts, feelings, and personalities.

   Change Corporate America to Advertisers.

   A) did already spent
   B) had spend
   C) was spending
   D) has spent
   E) spend

4) My grandfather told me that the secret to a happy life is to surround yourself with happy people.

   Start with The secret to a happy life.

   A) life, which was told to me by my grandfather, which is to
   B) is to surround yourself with happy people; according to what my grandfather told me.
   C) life, according to my grandfather,
   D) life, according to my grandfather; is to surround yourself with happy people
   E) my grandfather said to me to surround yourself with happy people.

5) Our generation was more concerned with spending quality time with family rather than spending our precious time at work.

Change Our generation to We.

A) is
B) are
C) have been
D) has been
E) can be

Revising Work in Progress

Directions: The following questions will test your ability to revise an early draft of an essay. The questions will refer to numbered sentences from the essay. You will be asked to improve sentence structure, diction (word choice), organization, development, and language in relation to purpose and audience.

QUESTIONS 1 TO 6 ARE BASED ON THE FOLLOWING PASSAGE.
(Passage 1)

(1) While government's role in individual choices should be limited, it is difficult to argue against government's involvement in helping Americans become and keep fit and healthy. (2) Encouraging Americans to maintain a lifestyle of health and fitness will have beneficial societal impact by reducing obesity-related diseases and health care costs and increase productivity. (3) By using existing government agencies such as public schools to educate children about nutrition and having daily and active physical education at the preschool level, and the President's "Fitness Program" to promote family fitness and healthy food and lifestyle choices. (4) Government, however, cannot be afraid to cite private enterprise products and services that are counter to living a fit and healthy lifestyle. (5) Including television watching (i.e. advertising) and often sedentary activity, eating processed foods and non-nutritious foods.

1) What is wrong with sentence 5?

   A) it is fine the way it is
   B) it is not relevant to the passage
   C) it is a run-on sentence
   D) it is a fragment
   E) it is a comma splice

2) How can sentences 4 and 5 be combined to create an effective sentence?

   A) It is fine the way it is.
   B) as it includes
   C) it includes
   D) lifestyle; this includes
   E) and includes

3) What type of passage is this?

   A) Illustrative
   B) Persuasive
   C) Descriptive
   D) Analytical
   E) Interpretive

4) What sentence is the thesis?

   A) 1
   B) 2
   C) 3
   D) 4
   E) 5

5) What is the purpose of sentences 3, 4, and 5?

   A) No purpose
   B) Supporting ideas for sentence 2
   C) Propaganda
   D) Comic relief
   E) Filler

6) The main implication of the passage is that?

   A) People shouldn't be controlled by government.
   B) Government should tell people what and what not to eat.
   C) Government has every right to keep Americans fit and healthy.
   D) Government can encourage Americans to be fit and healthy.
   E) The implication is not clear.

QUESTIONS 1 TO 5 ARE BASED ON THE FOLLOWING PASSAGE.

(Passage 2)

(1) The subject of poem number 508, by Emily Dickinson, is about being able to choose for herself now that she is an adult. (2) With a resentment towards her parents for baptizing her without a choice. (3) She feels that the name given to her as a baby is tainted and now that she is older she has no use for it because she has been "born again."

(4) The first clue of resentment toward her parents comes from how she talks of being baptized when she said they "dropped" the name on her face with water. (5) "Dropped" is a harsh word. (6) It implies that her parents were careless. (7) Then she said her name has no use now. (8) She talks of her name as if it's something you can just throw away like her childhood dolls and spools. (9) When she says she is finished threading, she means she is finished with her childhood in the way that her identity has changed as she has grown. (10) When she is finally able to choose for herself, there is a sense that she is relieved. (11) When she says, "this time, consciously of Grace," it's as if she feels free. (12) When she was baptized, she described herself as an "unconscious queen" who was crowned and crowing. (13) Crowned represents her baptism and crowing is her childhood, but then she says she has the will to choose or reject. (14) We can assume that she rejected her childhood and what was given her when she had no choice.

1) What purpose does sentence 11 serve?

   A) no purpose
   B) evidence for sentence 15
   C) support for sentence 7
   D) support for sentence 10
   E) to show how rebellious she is

2) What type of essay is this?

   A) Persuasive
   B) Analysis
   C) Narrative
   D) Argumentative
   E) Informative

3) Which is the best way to rewrite sentence 2?

   A) She has a resentment toward her parents for baptizing her when she couldn't choose for herself.
   B) She resents that her parents would baptize her without asking her.
   C) She resents being baptized.
   D) It is fine the way it is.
   E) Take the entire sentence out.

4) What sentence would logically start paragraph 2?

   A) 4
   B) 6
   C) 8
   D) 9
   E) 10

5) What sentence would logically start paragraph 3?

   A) 9
   B) 10
   C) 12
   D) 13
   E) 14

College Composition Modular

QUESTIONS 1 TO 5 ARE BASED ON THE FOLLOWING PASSAGE.

(Passage 3)

(1) As journalists, we have to be aware of bias in our writing, from other publications, and with ourselves because it is important to become more sensitive to things that others may be offended by. (2) Bias is not only found in words, but in headlines and photos and even where the story is placed in a publication. (3) Journalists may end up simplifying a story because they don't understand it so the story ends up one sided, biased, and unfair. (4) By using nonsexist language in the media we are taking an important step toward bias reduction. (5) Certain terms must be avoided because of their blatant implications. (6) For example, "man and wife," "male nurse," and "policeman" have obvious bias. (7) Eliminating these types of words from the media results in positive attitudes about the media as well as about other people. (8) There is a danger though when language seeks to be gender neutral. (9) This is a bias in itself, but there is something wrong when society tries to pretend there is no difference between men and women. (10) When language becomes too sterile, society denies real life.

1) What sentence would logically start paragraph 2?

   A) 2
   B) 3
   C) 4
   D) 6
   E) 7

2) What type of passage is this?

   A) Persuasive
   B) Informative
   C) Argumentative
   D) Illustrative
   E) Impressionistic

3) What should be done with sentences 8, 9, and 10?

   A) Leave it as it is.
   B) Omit sentence 10.
   C) Omit sentence 9.
   D) women, when
   E) Start a new paragraph with those sentences.

4) What sentence is the best thesis for this passage?

   A) 1
   B) 2
   C) 4
   D) 9
   E) 10

5) What should be done with the following part of sentence 1?
   in our writing, from other publications, and with ourselves.

   A) Leave it as it is.
   B) Omit it.
   C) in the media.
   D) in our writing, in other publications, and in ourselves.
   E) in our writing, publications, and with ourselves.

 # Analyzing Sentences

Directions: The following questions will test your ability to determine a writer's purpose and characteristics of prose. The questions will refer to numbered sentences based on a passage taken from only part of a complete writing sample.

QUESTIONS 1 TO 5 ARE BASED ON THE FOLLOWING PASSAGE.
(Passage 1)

(1) Most people would agree that Elizabeth Bennet is sensible and mature from the start of *Pride and Prejudice*, but she actually has two selves. (2) The first is the naïve and witty Lizzy at the beginning and the second is the aware and grown up Lizzy in the middle. (3) Elizabeth would like to think that her mother's shallow views never had any effect on her, but her mother as well as the rest of her family are all role models. (4) She wanted to believe that her opinion of Darcy as a proud and disagreeable man who as for respectability, "…he will probably never reach" was her own opinion. (5) It was not original though because, "When she thought of her mother indeed, her confidence gave way a little, but she would not allow that any objections there had material weight with Mr. Darcy, whose pride she was convinced, would receive a deeper wound from the want of importance in his friends' connections, than from their want of sense…". (6) Ultimately, Elizabeth changes from naïve to mature in her way of thinking when in her own experience she finally sees what her knowledgeable sister, Mary, knew all along and we see this change in two specific and related scenes.

1) What is the transitional phrase in sentence 6?

    A) There is no transitional phrase.
    B) knew all along
    C) she finally feels
    D) we see this change
    E) Ultimately

2) What is the purpose of sentence 1?

    A) to argue
    B) to show Elizabeth's weakness
    C) to gain credibility with the idea of the "two selves" statement
    D) a warm-up sentence
    E) to distract the reader

3) What type of passage is this?

   A) Informative
   B) Argumentative
   C) Impressionistic
   D) Persuasion
   E) Analytical

4) Sentences 4 and 5 serve what purpose?

   A) no purpose
   B) quotes to make Mr. Darcy look bad
   C) examples of opinions of Mr. Darcy
   D) examples of clear thinking
   E) examples of maturity

5) This passage portrays a theme of

   A) gossip
   B) ridicule
   C) maturity
   D) intelligence
   E) mental illness

QUESTIONS 1 TO 5 ARE BASED ON THE FOLLOWING PASSAGE.

(Passage 2)

(1) In a *Midsummer Night's Dream* we can laugh at the trials and tribulations of love because as Puck said, "That you have but slumbered here (too)." (2) It's funny to see how other people are blind when they are in love, but it's not so funny when it happens to us. (3) For the characters in the play, these things are not so amusing. (4) Lysander, Hermia, Demetrius, and Helena belong to two worlds. (5) One world exists in reality which is ruled by Theseus and the other world exists in fantasy which is ruled by Oberon. (6) The four lovers get caught up in the fantasy world where they battle with the rational mind of which Theseus preaches and the passion of love which also takes over Titania and has already affected Theseus (though he would never admit it). (7) Titania and Theseus's example show us that headstrong love can happen to anyone and the four lovers go through the cycle of love where they are passionate before they are reasonable.

1) What sentence is the thesis?

   A) 1
   B) 2
   C) 5
   D) 6
   E) 7

2) What is the best revision of sentence 2?

   A) It is fine the way it is.
   B) It's funny when people are in love because they are blind.
   C) It's funny to watch people being blinded by love, but it is not so funny when it is happening to us.
   D) We have been in love before and it sure is funny.
   E) Remove the whole sentence.

3) What purpose does the quoted text serve in sentence 1?

   A) serves no purpose
   B) provides comic relief
   C) to evoke common experience in the reader
   D) a chance to put fancy words in an essay
   E) to evoke sleep in the reader

4) What do the words in parentheses signify in sentence 6?

   A) signifies nothing
   B) can't tell from the passage
   C) gives us a glimpse into his stubbornness
   D) he is secretive
   E) he doesn't know what is going on

5) Sentence 7 is setting the reader up for

   A) disappointment.
   B) an essay on love.
   C) paragraphs that show each character's experience in the cycle of love.
   D) paragraphs that show relationship that Titania and Theseus have.
   E) a book report on a Midsummer Night's Dream.

Essay Writing

The best way to prepare for the essay writing portion of the CLEP examination is to practice writing. You will be writing the essay portion of the exam on a computer. This study guide will explain the structure you will need to follow when writing an essay. You will have 35 minutes to write two essays on a given subject. Only write an essay on the given topic in the exam. If you write an essay on a topic you create, it will not be accepted. At least five minutes will be spent thinking about the topic and how you will write about it. Practicing writing an essay within a 35-minute time schedule will reduce any anxiety you may otherwise experience at test time. There is no need for this anxiety. Try using the following essay tips for writing a practice essay. Choose a topic from the list in this study guide.

ESSAY EXAM WRITING TIPS:

An excellent essay will have:

- a clear thesis
- everything in the paper related to the thesis
- clear organization
- appropriate connection between sentences and paragraphs
- a strong style
- command of grammar, punctuation, and mechanics
- no spelling errors

Be alert to the following instruction key words that you may come across in exam questions. If the question asks you to analyze something, it doesn't mean the same thing as defining it. These terms are not used interchangeably.

analyze	examine critically in order to bring out the essential elements of
apply	make use of as relevant or to apply a theory to a problem
assess	estimate, evaluate, or judge the value of
compare	examine two or more things in order to note similarities and differences
contrast	compare in order to show unlikeness or differences; to show the opposite qualities of
define	give the meaning of
demonstrate	explain or illustrate by example; establish by reasoning
describe	give a detailed account; list characteristics, qualities, and parts
determine	decide upon; conclude or ascertain after reasoning or observation

discuss	consider and debate or argue the pros and cons of an issue; compare and contrast
distinguish	indicate or show a difference between
enumerate	list several ideas, aspects, events, things, qualities, reasons, etc.
explain	make clear the cause or reason of; to make known in detail
generalize	form a general opinion or conclusion from only a few facts or cases
illustrate	give concrete examples; explain clearly by using comparisons or examples
interpret	comment upon, give examples, describe relationships; describe, then evaluate
justify	show or prove to be just, right, or reasonable
list	items written in a series that creates a meaningful grouping or sequence
outline	describe main ideas, characteristics, or events (different from a Roman numeral/letter outline)
prove	support with facts
rank	make orderly arrangements of items
show	explain what is meant
summarize	write a brief and comprehensive recap of previous statements

 Strategy for Writing the Entire Essay

Take a look at this online writing assistant site for essays http://www.powa.org/

1. Make sure your first paragraph contains your thesis statement. A thesis is a sentence that states the main point or idea of the essay. The thesis will give your essay direction. If the essay topic is controversial, the first paragraph is also where you will either agree with or disagree with the statement. In both cases, you will have to use supporting evidence. The side you choose has nothing to do with the score you receive. You will be scored on your ability to organize and write effectively.

2. Think of at least three supporting factors for your thesis and expand on those ideas with examples or illustrations. Each supporting factor should have its own paragraph. Use the scratch paper provided to write outlines or ideas.

Useful transitions to illustrate an idea:
For example, To illustrate, For instance, In this manner, In particular, Thus

3. The last paragraph will be your conclusion. Your conclusion will be a summary of the points you have made on your thesis. Do not add a new idea in your conclusion. This is the time to give your essay positive closure with the last sentence. The reader, in this case the grader, should not feel abandoned in the last paragraph. Don't give your essay that dreaded unfinished feeling. The thesis gives your paper direction, but it has to end smoothly too.

Useful transitions for your conclusion:
In short, On the whole, To conclude, In brief, To sum up

4. It is easy to get off the subject of your thesis. Make sure you stay on track by reading your thesis after you write each paragraph.
5. The organizational style of your essay should be uncomplicated and straightforward.
6. If you have time, reread the paper when you are finished to look for:
   - Misspelled words
   - Omitted words
   - Incorrect grammar and punctuation
   - Incorrect dates and figures

STRATEGY FOR WRITING EACH PARAGRAPH

TRIAC: Paragraph and Paper Organization
TRIAC is a writing strategy you can use for each paragraph to create a solid organization and an effective argument. TRIAC stands for:

T	Topic Sentence - The first sentence introduces the subject of a paragraph, and serves as a "minor" thesis statement.
R	Restatement or Restriction - The second sentence can restate or restrict what was written in the first sentence, making the subject more specific.
I	Illustration - This section of the paragraph consists of the illustrations (evidence, data, facts, quotes, etc.) that support your topic sentence. This section can contain several sentences.

A	Analysis - Explain, interpret, and contextualize the illustrations that have been made. Illustrations are not effective without the writer analyzing them.
C	Conclusion - The final sentence (or two) might review what the paragraph has discussed, and/or reemphasize what the illustration and analysis suggest. This closing section may also evaluate the connections you've made in your paragraph. You are setting yourself up to move smoothly and logically into the next paragraph.

5 x 5 Paragraph Essay

A 5x5 paragraph essay is one of the most basic forms of essay writing. It breaks the essay down into five sections: the introduction, three body paragraphs, and the conclusion. Each section should contain five sentences. For the introduction paragraph, the first line should be the thesis. The thesis is followed by three supporting statements, and the final line leads into the next paragraph. The three body paragraphs all follow the same format, with the first line taken from the supporting statements from the introduction paragraph (the first supporting statement starts paragraph two, the second starts paragraph three, and the third starts paragraph four). Each body paragraph should then contain three supporting statements and a concluding line which links to the next paragraph. The concluding paragraph should start with a line summarizing the point of the essay, have three sentences restating the original supporting lines, and then restate the thesis.

Practice Essay Topics

Use some of the following topics to write essays or create your own essay topic.

(Try practicing writing an essay on a computer since the essay portion of the exam will also be on a computer.)

a) The images of children currently portrayed in the media are accurately depicted from today's youth. Agree or disagree.

b) Euthanizing animals in humane societies is actually not humane. Agree or disagree.

c) Explain what you think have been the main reasons for the increase in violent behavior in our schools.

d) Discuss changes that might occur if milk prices go up to $5.00 a gallon.

e) If you could influence the way products are advertised in the United States, what recommendations, if any, would you make? Discuss.

f) There should be a law restricting ownership of dangerous pets such as pit bulldogs. Agree or disagree.

g) The elderly are a precious resource that the United States is wasting. Agree or disagree.

h) Archaeologists have learned much about the lives of first-century Romans from the excavations of houses buried by lava at Pompeii. Suppose that your home were preserved just as it is now. What conclusions about modern life might future archaeologists draw from this evidence?

Formats and Documentation

When you "cite" a source, your instructor will tell you whether he wants MLA (Modern Language Association) form, APA (American Psychological Association) form, or another style. While the styles of documentation differ, the basics are the same.

1) A bibliography will be required
   A bibliography is a list of all the sources you used to find your facts. Depending on the style of documentation, a bibliography will be called either "Works Cited" or "Reference" page. This page is the final page of your paper. Its purpose is to have complete publication information on each source so that if a reader found an interesting fact that she'd like to read more about in the body of the paper, she could turn to the bibliography to find exact publication information.
   Each source that you utilized will be listed with these three essential groupings of information:

   a) Author
   b) Title of work
   c) Publication data (dates, publisher, page numbers)

2) Each time you use a fact, idea, statistic, quote, or theory from an outside source, you must cite it in parentheses. "Citing it" means that you'll include vital information like the author, the date, and/or the page number from which you found that fact in parentheses immediately after the fact. (What you'll include in the parentheses depends on whether you're using MLA or APA or another format.) The information given in parentheses is an abbreviation of the complete information listed on the bibliography page. The brief information in the parentheses enables

the reader to cross-reference the source to the complete publication information at the end of the paper. This kind of documentation takes the place of the old-fashioned footnotes and is called "parenthetical citation" or "in-text citation."

3) Some general rules about parenthetical citation:

   a) The author's last name is always the first part of a citation.
   b) If there is no listed author, the title of the article is used.
   c) No punctuation appears before the beginning of the parentheses.
   d) The only period for the sentence is placed AFTER the citation.

4) Some general rules about bibliographies:

   a) First part of any entry is the last name of the author.
   b) If no author is listed, use the title of the article or book.
   c) All entries are alphabetized by the author's last name or the first major word of the title.
   d) Bibliography pages have a heading in the top right corner, including a final page number.
   e) Forms are VERY specific with different punctuation and ordering applying to different types of sources. Be sure to check with your instructor about the appropriate form to use and then follow the guidelines for the selected style.

What about footnotes and end notes? What are they and how to they work? They are those little numbers you see while reading a book or a document like this[1]. Footnotes and endnotes basically do the same job. What is different about them is their placement. The information about a resource for footnotes are at the bottom or end of a page. Endnotes are at the end of a chapter, book, or document. Both of these notation types are used to give the reader information about the source material of a certain section.

History is written by a process of argument. A good argument puts forward a point of view that is well grounded: it has evidence to support it. Unlike practitioners of other fields such as engineering or the natural sciences, historians pose questions that rarely have definitive answers or solutions. The emphasis in history is on an analysis of past events using a variety of historical evidence. Because much of the historian's task is interpretative, there are strict requirements regarding the correct citation of sources. Scholars use footnotes and/or endnotes for a variety of reasons including:

- To make it clear to the reader which views are yours and which are the views of other writers;
- To allow you to acknowledge your intellectual debts to others if you decide to accept their views or information;

- To direct the reader by the most efficient signposts to the place where the information you have provided can be checked and verified or where further useful information is.

Correspondingly, there are a number of situations where you MUST cite your sources.

- Direct quotations
- Any material that has been paraphrased from an outside source
- Any reference to arguments or facts (i.e. budget figures, technical specifications) that have been garnered from an outside source

There are also circumstances in which you SHOULD footnote

- To provide the reader with a guide to the sources used in the formation of the author's original argument.
- To provide the reader with a guide to sources that offer further information on ideas or arguments summarized in the author's text.
- To offer the reader further details or discussion beyond what could be reasonably included in the main text.
- If information is not common knowledge to the average lay reader.

Number of Notes

- If there is more than one sentence in a single paragraph that requires a footnote you may consolidate these by putting multiple sources in a single note and the end of the paragraph. If you choose to do this, you MUST arrange the sources in the footnote to correspond to the appropriate sentences in your text. You must also explain any potential ambiguities about which source refers to what information within the paragraph.
- You should NEVER use one footnote to refer to material in more than a single paragraph of text.
- So for each paragraph, you should ask yourself the following question: What primary and/or secondary sources did I use in the creation of this paragraph?

Web Citations

- While it is acceptable to cite electronic sources (emails, Web sites, online journals, online databases, etc.), if it is at all possible we would prefer to have the reference to the original material that was used in the creation of the electronic document.

- When referencing a Web site, it is imperative that the author include the date that the site was accessed online in the citation. In addition, the author needs to print out the electronic document for inclusion in the appropriate Historical Reference Collection. These precautionary steps ensure that if an ephemeral Web site disappears later, there will still be a record of the content material.

- Please do NOT cite on-line encyclopedias such as Wikipedia for several reasons. First, Wikipedia does not list the author or creator of the information. Second, its content changes frequently. Third, encyclopedias usually contain factual information. (If you don't know certain facts, it's obviously fine to look them anywhere you choose, but facts typically do NOT need to be footnoted.)

How to Cite a Newspaper vs. Book

Two commonly cited references are newspaper articles and books. The two have similar citations, but it is important that they are done correctly. For a book, the format is:

Author. *Title of Book*. City of Publication: Publisher, Year. Print.

The author should be listed last name, first name. If there are multiple authors only the first needs to be reversed. The title of the book should be taken from the title page (not the cover). The word print indicates that it was accessed as a printed source. The format for a newspaper is:

Author. "Title of Article." *Name of Newspaper* Date, edition: Page(s). Print.

Just as with a book the author's name should be reversed and separated by a comma, and the name of the newspaper is italicized. Notice that the name of the newspaper and the date are not separated by any punctuation.

 *Reference Skills*

Wouldn't it be nice if you typed the subject of your research paper into the computer and it gave you a list of sources that were perfectly suited to your topic?

It would be nice, but it wouldn't be realistic! Sources are catalogued in many different ways and with very different words. Here are some guidelines for making "research" go a little more smoothly:

1. Check the <u>Library of Congress Subject Heading Index</u>: This book will give you examples of the keywords used in categorizing your topic. Knowing how your topic is described by librarians and cataloguers saves you lots of time and increases the accuracy of your "hits."

2. Start up your engines! Search engines are tools which peruse the internet for information on your requested topic. Since all search engines are organized and indexed differently, it's a good idea to try more than one search engine to retrieve information on your topic. Some of the better known search engines are Google, Alta Vista, Excite, HotBot, InfoSeek, Lycos, and Yahoo.

3. Old-Fashioned but Worthy: While many indexes are online, you can also still go to the old fashioned print catalogues at your local library. <u>The Reader's Guide to Periodicals</u> indexes all the magazine articles that have appeared in the popular press for any given year. Learn how to use it because although many things are available in computer databases and retrievable through search engines, that information is often no more than a few years old. If you are doing historical research, or looking for perspectives on an incident that happened long ago, you will most likely have success in the print sources.

4. Specialized Indexes: Many magazines have specialized indexes which, again, are of great help in researching historical topics. Many of these indexes are indexed for the most recent years online. Check out the hard copy and the online versions of magazines like <u>National Geographic</u>, <u>American History Illustrated</u>, and <u>The Journal of American Medical Association</u>.

5. Indexes to <u>New York Times</u> and <u>Chicago Tribune</u>: Even though these are newspapers, they are NATIONAL newspapers covering all kinds of news, including historical topics.

6. Databases: Many libraries offer access to online databases. Check out services like InfoTrac, FirstSearch, Wilson's Select Plus, ERIC, and others. Articles and essays found in electronic databases are acceptable resources! Make sure you understand the difference between a database and a website. A database pools all kinds of previously published articles and essays from magazines and journals

all over the world. This means that the information is more credible because you have a specific author, a specific publication, and a specific date. In other words, an article pulled out of a database has a "print analogue."

Use of Reference Books

When you do utilize reference books, you need to be able to understand the functions and the purposes of the books and their varying sections.

1. Encyclopedias: Most college-level instructors do not allow students to copy facts from encyclopedias. However, encyclopedias can aid researchers in supplying helpful bibliographies and the names of recognized authorities.
2. Textbooks and Reference Manuals: Used for substantive data and theory, textbooks and reference manuals are very thorough, but often out-of-date as soon as they are printed.
3. Glossaries: Often found at the back of textbooks, glossaries are specialized dictionaries that define the terms used in this particular field.
4. Indexes: Specialized publications focusing on one particular topic or field. For instance, there are indexes for medical topics, for business topics, for literary criticism, and for film reviews. Such indexes give the precise publication data for articles that appeared on that topic.

Footnotes and Endnotes

Footnotes and endnotes are used to give the bibliographic information of works cited in the body of a document. When using note style documentation, a number is written as a superscript after the information that is cited. If the paper uses footnotes, the numbers and the corresponding bibliographic entries for each page are listed four lines after the last line of text on the page. In endnote documentation, all of the notes are listed in a supplement to the paper. In both footnote and endnote notations, the citations are labeled chronologically according to how they appear in the text.

The form an endnote or footnote takes depends on the type of material being cited. Enough information should be included to allow the reader to find the source material if more information is needed. Table 8 shows note documentation styles for some common types of material.

Examples of Footnotes

Description of Source Material	Example Citation Notes
Book written by one author	[1] Patricia Larkins Hicks, <u>Opportunities in Speech-Language Pathology Careers</u> (New York: McGraw Hill, 2007) 93. [2] Dorothy P. Dougherty, <u>Teach Me How to Say It Right</u> (Oakland: New Harbinger, 2005) 54.
Book written by two or more authors	[3] Froma P. Roth and Collen K. Worthington, <u>Treatment Resource Manual for Speech-Language Pathology</u> (Albany: Delmar, 2001) 201.
Edited book	[4] Lee Edward Travis, ed., <u>Handbook of Speech Pathology</u> (New York: Apple Century Crofts, 1957) 8.
Magazine article	[5] Craig Boerner, "Sleep Levels in Children with ASD," <u>Advance for Speech-Language Pathologists and Audiologists</u> 17.49 (2007):14.

In some academic disciplines, parenthetical documentation is preferred over footnotes and endnotes for citing sources. In parenthetical documentation styles, the source is identified in the body of the paper. For example:

> A hyphen is used to form compound words such as great-uncle (Stoughton 150).

The in-text documentation refers the reader to the appropriate entry in the paper's bibliography. The citation includes the author or editor's last name and the page number from which the information was taken.

If the paper drew information from more than one work by the same author, the citation should include a key word from the title of the appropriate source. Just enough information is required to help the reader identify the right source.

In the following example, the citation sends the reader to page 85 of Harbrace College Handbook edited by John Hodges. Just enough information is included in the citation to allow the reader to find the correct entry in the bibliography or list of works cited.

> The past participle form of the verb *to spit* is *spat* (Hodges, Handbook 85).

When parenthetical documentation is used, the complete bibliographic information for each work cited should be included at the end of the paper.
Footnotes and endnotes may also be used to provide supplemental information about the material discussed in the body of the document. Common uses for background notes in technical documents include:

- Explanations for missing or anomalous data in graphs, tables, or charts.
- Information tangential to the topic of the paper but of probable interest to the reader.
- Minor details about methodology that might influence a process's repeatability.

The example below shows how footnotes can be used to provide background information in a technical document.

Using Background Footnotes

> We decided to use the test field at Cooper's Ridge after the soil tests at the other sites showed high alkalinity.[1] We divided the test field into eight sections and divided different concentrations of the herbicide to each section. The number of visible *Viola papilionacea* clusters and the average number of leaves from a random sampling of clusters at each site was measured 1, 2, 3, 4, and 6 days after application.[2]
>
> [1] Although current research suggests the pH of the soil would have little or no influence on the herbicide's effectiveness, at the time it seemed important to test the compound on a soil with a chemical composition as close to that found at the Glen Oaks subdivision as possible.
> [2] Measurements were not taken on the fifth day after herbicide application because a rock slide on the highway blocked access to the test field.

Notes used to give background information should not be mixed with notes used for source citations. Background and bibliographic notes may be distinguished by using numerical superscripts for one type and alphabetical superscripts for the other. Alternatively, background notes may be used with parenthetical source documentation.

 Word Choice and Idiom Review

COMMONLY MISUSED WORDS

Knowing the different meanings of words can help you at exam time. Below are some commonly misused words and idiomatic prepositional phrases. It's a good idea to review more than this list. If you see words like these on the examination, a red flag should go up in your mind and you should check if it is the correct use of the word. *For more misused words try this site http://www.bartleby.com/141/strunk3.html*

Accept	to receive
Except	to exclude
Affect (vb.)	to influence, to change
Effect	to accomplish (vb.); a result (n.)
All right	correct spelling
Alright	incorrect spelling
Among	when referring to more than two
Between	when referring to only two
Continual	recurring actions, repeated regularly and frequently
Continuous	occurring without interruption
Disinterested	impartial
Uninterested	not interested
Emigrate	one emigrates *from* a place
Immigrate	one immigrates *to* a place
Eminent	outstanding, distinguished
Imminent	threatening to happen soon
Ensure	to guarantee; to make safe
Insure	to provide insurance against loss
Farther	describes distance
Further	additionally; suggests quantity or degree

Fewer	used when nouns can be counted and made plural (fewer students)
Less	used when nouns can't be counted or made plural (less homework)
Good	an adjective before a noun or after a linking verb (look good)
Well	an adverb when referring to how an action is performed
Respectfully	courteously
Respectively	each in the order given
Set	to put or to place
Sit	to be seated
Unquestionable	indisputable
Unquestioned	has not been questioned

COMMONLY MISUSED IDIOMATIC PREPOSITIONAL PHRASES

Agree on, Agree to, Agree with: *Everyone* will *agree on* the matter. They will *agree to* the proposition. I *agree with* your statement.

Argue about, Argue for: He *argues about* everything. He *argued for* implementing dolphin-safe tuna.

Disappointed by, Disappointed in, Disappointed with: She is *disappointed by* her brother who let her down. She is *disappointed in* her insignificant raise. They are *disappointed with* the low sales figures.

Live at, Live in, Live on: You *live at* the house on the corner. You *live in* Illinois. You *live on* Ewing Avenue.

Exam Tips

1) Pay attention to the following words in test questions. These key words will reveal whether there are no exceptions or some exceptions to the answer.

No Exceptions	Some Exceptions
always	often
every	rarely
all	sometimes
only	generally
never	usually
none	seldom
not	however
must	perhaps
necessary	but
	except
	may

2) Read the test directions carefully. You can never be absolutely certain of what the test wants you to do without reading the directions first.

3) Try to answer each test item before reading the answer choices. If you see your answer among the choices, select it right away.

4) If you don't know the answer until you read the choices and then notice the correct answer, select it without thinking twice.

5) If you really aren't sure of the answer to any test item, go on to the next one and come back to it later. The test item will usually seem clearer when you come back to it and the answer will be easier to spot.

6) If you decide to come back to a test item, be alert and leave that item number blank on the answer sheet so you don't accidentally fill in the answer for the next item in that space.

7) Do not change your answers after you have selected them. Your first guess is more likely to be correct than subsequent guesses.

8) If you have tried all of the above steps and you simply do not know the answer, then make an educated guess. You will not be penalized for incorrect answers.

9) This exam tests a lot of what you should have already learned in high school. Therefore, knowing what to expect by reading this study guide and reviewing other resources will be to your advantage.

Study Guide Answer Key

IDENTIFYING SENTENCE ERRORS

Pronouns

1. **A** whom should be who
2. **C** I should be me
3. **C** of me should be of my
4. **A** who's should be whose
5. **B** it's should be its
6. **C** whomever should be whoever
7. **E** no error
8. **E** no error

Agreement of Subject and Verb

1. **A** is should be are
2. **D** they choose should be it chooses
3. **B** media are should be media is
4. **D** was should be were
5. **E** no error

Word Choices, Diction, and Idioms

1. **C** affects should be effects
2. **A** of should be have
3. **C** capitol should be capital
4. **A** good should be well
5. **B** relationship should be correlation
6. **A** between should be among

Parallelism

1. C
2. E
3. C
4. C
5. D

Dangling and Misplaced Modifiers

1. **D**
2. **A**
3. **D**
4. **D**
5. **D**

Verb Forms

1. **B** become used
2. **A** had fallen
3. **C** had taken
4. **C** had drunk
5. **C** had encountered

Sentence Problems

1. **D**
2. **A**
3. **A**
4. **E**
5. **D**

Improving Sentences

1. **B**
2. **C**
3. **B**
4. **D**
5. **D**

Restructuring Sentences

1. **C**
2. **A**
3. **E**
4. **C**
5. **C**

Revising Work in Progress

(Passage 1)
1. D
2. D
3. B
4. B
5. B
6. D

Revising Work in Progress

(Passage 2)
1. D
2. B
3. A
4. A
5. B

(Passage 3)
1. C
2. B
3. E
4. A
5. D

Analyzing Writing

(Passage 1)
1. E
2. C
3. E
4. C
5. C

(Passage 2)
1. E
2. C
3. C
4. C
5. C

 # Additional Practice Test

I. *PUNCTUATION*

CHOOSE THE LETTER IN FRONT OF THE BEST SENTENCE.

1)
- A) GM had started production of the cars in 1995 it was fully aware of the brake problems.
- B) GM had started production of the cars in 1995; it was fully aware of the brake problems.
- C) GM had started production of the cars in 1995, it was fully aware of the brake problems.
- D) GM had started production of the cars in 1995: it was fully aware of the brake problems.
- E) GM had started production of the cars in 1995, although it was fully aware of the brake problems.

2)
- A) GM recalled 48,000 cars in 1998 that recall did not solve the problem
- B) GM recalled 48,000 cars in 1998 however that recall did not solve the problem.
- C) GM recalled 48,000 cars in 1998, that recall did not solve the problem.
- D) GM recalled 48,000 cars in 1998, although that recall did not solve the problem.
- E) GM recalled 48,000 cars in 1998, but that recall did not solve the problem.

3)
- A) Many people laughed at Kuhn, because he wore a suit and necktie to ballgames.
- B) Because he wore a suit and necktie to ballgames many people laughed at Kuhn.
- C) Because he wore a suit and necktie to ballgames, many people laughed at Kuhn.
- D) Because he wore a suit and necktie to ballgames; many people laughed at Kuhn.
- E) He wore a suit and necktie to ballgames as a result many people laughed at him.

4)
- A) Our class visited a water witch because we wanted to learn this art.
- B) Herman used forked sticks from Chinese elm trees, traditionally, willow sticks are used.
- C) Because water witching is a folk science; many people look on it with suspicion.
- D) He holds the stick by the forked end, and walks up and down on a piece of ground.
- E) He holds the stick by the forked end; and walks up and down on a piece of ground.

5)
- A) Dogs, that come in many sizes, are popular pets.
- B) Wolves, which were originally found all over Europe, are the ancestors of dogs.
- C) Wolves' tails turn downward; although dogs' tails turn upward.
- D) Dogs were domesticated all over the world, and were even owned by Indians.
- E) Wolves found all Europe, are the ancestors of dogs.

II. *COMBINED SENTENCES*

CHOOSE THE LETTER IN FRONT OF THE BEST SENTENCE.

1)
- A) Helen Murphy is crippled; therefore, she uses a wheel chair.
- B) Her wheelchair is electric-powered, it also has a fringed canopy.
- C) Because pedestrians complained to the police; she was taken to court.
- D) Although the pedestrians are safe through the week the Sunday morning joggers had better watch out.
- E) The pedestrians are safe through the week, although the Sunday morning joggers had better watch out.

2)
- A) Henry James wrote a story called *The Turn of the Screw* in fact the story has nothing to do with carpentry
- B) Henry James wrote a story called *The Turn of the Screw*; however, the story has nothing to do with carpentry.
- C) Henry James wrote a story called *The Turn of the Screw* but the story has nothing to do with carpentry.
- D) Henry James wrote a story called *The Turn of the Screw* still the story has nothing to do with carpentry.
- E) Henry James wrote a story called *The Turn of the Screw*; although the story has nothing to do with carpentry.

3)
   A) Although the man employs her he never sees her again.
   B) Although the man employs her, he never sees her again.
   C) The man never sees her again, although he had employed her.
   D) The man never sees her again; although he had employed her.
   E) The man never sees her again however he had employed her.

4)
   A) Eighteen people have contracted the plague in New Mexico this year as a matter of fact there are more cases than in any state since 1925.
   B) Because there is a sever outbreak there this year several people have died of the plague
   C) Several people have died of the plague in New Mexico, because there is a severe outbreak there this year.
   D) Until the cause of the plague is found people will continue to die.
   E) Eighteen people have contracted the plague in New Mexico this year; as a matter of fact, there are more cases than in any state since 1925.

5)
   A) Dragonflies have large eyes, that look like jewels.
   B) Dragonflies have large eyes which look like jewels.
   C) Dragonflies have large eyes that look like jewels.
   D) Dragonflies have large eyes; which look like jewels.
   E) Dragonflies have large eyes in fact they look like jewels.

III. *POSSESSIVES*

CHOOSE THE LETTER IN FRONT OF THE BEST SENTENCE.

1)
   A) The worlds highest mountain peaks have long been a challenge to mountain climbers.
   B) Most mountain peaks' in the United States can be climbed during a weekends vacation.
   C) Most mountain peaks in the United States can be climbed during a weekends vacation.
   D) The origin of mountain climbing seems to be tied to peoples' religious experiences.
   E) The Alps have always been European climbers' favorite area.

2)
- A) The ancient Greeks and Romans thought that their gods' home was on Mount Olympus.
- B) Mount Rainier and the Grand Teton are the United State's most popular mountains.
- C) The World Book Encyclopedias' sponsorship led to a famous climb by Hillary.
- D) Two of Hillarys' books are especially fascinating to those whose passion is mountain climbing.
- E) Two of Hillarys books are especially fascinating to those whose passion is mountain climbing.

3)
- A) Ichabod Cranes student's took revenge because he punished them.
- B) Brom Bones drawing of Ichabod made the teacher very angry.
- C) Brom's horses name was Gunpowder.
- D) Brom's horse's name was Gunpowder.
- E) Ichabod Cranes' students took revenge because he punished them.

4)
- A) Jody said that the drawing was her's.
- B) The Browns were proud of their new car.
- C) The three girls insisted that the money was their's.
- D) "Is it you'res," asked Mrs. Barberry.
- E) "Is it your's," asked Mrs. Barberry.

5)
- A) The dog was beautiful; I especially liked it's coat.
- B) The puppy's favorite activity was chasing its tail.
- C) After we started the tutoring program, some of our students test scores improved dramatically.
- D) Although I bought my daughter clothes in the latest style, she preferred last years' faded, ragged jeans.
- E) Although I bought my daughter clothes in the latest style, she preferred last years faded, ragged jean's.

IV. SUBORDINATION AND COORDINATION

IN THE FOLLOWING SENTENCES, CHOOSE THE SENTENCE THAT DOES NOT HAVE A SUBORDINATION OR COORDINATION FAULT.

1)
   A) He is a person of great integrity, talent, and has the rare combination of drive and commitment that leads to success in the business world.
   B) He is a person of great integrity and talent and has the rare combination of drive and commitment that leads to success in the business world.
   C) He is a person of great integrity, talent, rare combination of drive and commitment that leads to success in the business world.
   D) He is a person of great integrity, talent, and is the rare combination of drive and commitment that leads to success in the business world.
   E) He is a person of great integrity, talent, but is the rare combination of drive and commitment that leads to success in the business world.

2)
   A) The players on the college team were skillful, prepared, but less committed than their counterparts on the high-school team.
   B) The players on the college team were skillful, prepared, and less committed than their counterparts on the high-school team.
   C) The players on the college team were more skillful, better prepared, less committed than their counterparts on the high-school team.
   D) The players on the college team were more skillful and better prepared; however, they were less committed than their counterparts on the high-school team.
   E) The players on the college team were skillful, prepared, less committed than their counterparts on the high-school team.

3)
   A) From the airplane, the river seemed languid, serene, and tranquilly flowed toward the sea.
   B) From the airplane, the river seemed languid, serene, and tranquil as it flowed toward the sea.
   C) From the airplane, the river seemed languid, serene, and tranquilly flowing toward the sea.
   D) From the airplane, the river seemed languid, serene and flowed tranquilly toward the sea.
   E) The river seemed languid, serene, tranquilly flowing toward the sea and could be seen from the airplane.

4)
   A) To hike the Appalachian Trail, one needs to be knowledgeable about survival as well as excellent physical condition.
   B) To hike the Appalachian Trail, one needs to be knowledgeable about survival, and should be in excellent physical condition.
   C) To hike the Appalachian Trail, one needs to be knowledgeable about survival and should be in excellent physical condition.
   D) To hike the Appalachian Trail, one needs to be knowledgeable about survival, be in excellent physical condition.
   E) To hike the Appalachian Trail, one needs to be knowledgeable about survival, and excellent physical condition.

5)
   A) Janie's professor told her that she should find a better place to study, she needed to spend less time visiting with her friends, and ought to attend class more frequently.
   B) Janie's professor told her that she should find a better place to study, she needed to spend less time visiting with her friends, and she ought to attend class more frequently.
   C) Janie's professor told her that she should find a better place to study, less time visiting with her friends, and ought to attend class more frequently.
   D) Janie's professor told her that she should find a better place to study, spend less time visiting with her friends, and she ought to attend class more frequently.
   E) Janie's professor told her that she should find a better place to study, spend less time visiting with her friends, and she might try to attend class more frequently.

V. *IDENTIFYING SENTENCE ERRORS*

IDENTIFY THE ERROR IN THE FOLLOWING SENTENCES.

Some are correct, and no sentence contains more than one error. The error, if there is one, is underlined and lettered. The elements in the sentence that are not underlined are correct. If there is no error, select answer E.

1) People <u>who hike</u> the Appalachian Trail <u>may stay</u> <u>overnight</u> in shelters if <u>you
        A   B   C   D
   choose</u>. <u>No error</u>.
                    E

2) <u>College Professor #11</u> <u>teaches</u> <u>their children</u> <u>to write</u> biographies. <u>No error</u>.
              A   B   C   D   E

3) His son <u>grew up</u> <u>to become</u> a successful doctor, author, soccer <u>coach, and</u> have <u>a</u>
       A   B   C   D
   <u>very successful</u> family life. <u>No error</u>.
                                        E

4) <u>My mother was</u> a very special woman <u>with extraordinary talents</u> <u>who made</u> a
         A   B   C
   comfortable home <u>and was</u> a gracious host. <u>No error</u>.
                        D   E

5) <u>Convinced</u> <u>that</u> our community was not <u>well-informed</u> about the issues, <u>pamphlets</u>
         A   B   C
   <u>were printed</u> <u>about the program</u>. <u>No error</u>.
         D   E

VI. *IMPROVING SENTENCES*

In the following sentences, part of the sentence or all of the sentence is underlined. There are five versions of the underlined part. Choice A repeats the original; the other three are different. Choose the answer that best expresses the intended meaning. Choice A may be the correct one. Choose the one that makes the most effective sentence without awkwardness or ambiguity.

1) They associate <u>pain to being a hyper-consumer and pleasure to being frugal</u>.

   A) pain to being a hyper-consumer and pleasure to being frugal.
   B) pain with being a hyper-consumer and pleasure to being frugal.
   C) pain to being a hyper-consumer and pleasure with being frugal.
   D) pain with being a hyper-consumer and pleasure with being frugal.
   E) pain because being a hyper-consumer and pleasure to being frugal.

2) The reason I don't approve of research projects in schools <u>is because we must protect our liberties</u>.

   A) is because we must protect our liberties.
   B) ; however, we must protect our liberties.
   C) is that we must protect our liberties.
   D) is that, we must protect our liberties.
   E) is for we must protect our liberties.

3) In this day and age the problem of smoking marijuana has had a much freer scope in recent years than was the case at an earlier period in time.

   A) In this day and age the problem of smoking marijuana has had a much freer scope in recent years than was the case at an earlier period in time.
   B) Smoking marijuana is not as severely condemned as it once was.
   C) The problem of smoking marijuana has a much freer scope nowadays than it used to have.
   D) Today, the problem of smoking marijuana is more accepted than was the case at an earlier period of time.
   E) The problem of smoking marijuana is more accepted than was the case at an earlier period in time.

4) All the girls were looked on as a sister in the camp.

   A) as a sister in the camp.
   B) as sisters in the camp.
   C) like a sister in the camp.
   D) being a sister in the camp.
   E) To be a sister in the camp.

5) Although there are many faults in the administration of the school, there are not enough to justify a change.

   A) Although there are many faults in the administration of the school, there are not enough to justify a change.
   B) There are not enough faults to justify a change in the administration of the school, although there are many faults.
   C) Although there are many faults in the administration of the school, there are not enough to make it an unprofitable change.
   D) There are many faults in the administration of the school, therefore a change is justified.
   E) There are many faults in the administration of the school there are not enough to justify a change.

VII. *IMPROVING SENTENCES*

The following is a draft of a student composition with the sentences numbered for reference. Read the essay and then answer the questions that follow. You will be improving these sentences to solve problems in structure, usage, and diction.

(1) The truth is most people are a combination of their met programs and internal and external frames. (2) However, if a child becomes too externally framed, they will be influenced by whatever the crowd is doing. (3) The problem with this type of thinking is the average person in the crowd is barely paying their bills and certainly not a success. (4) If Thomas Edison was an external thinker do you think he would have discovered the light bulb? (5) If John F. Kennedy was externally framed, do you think he would have ordered a military blockade against Cuba. (6) Or do you think he would have listened to Kruschev and allowed Soviet nuclear sites to be permanently established 90 miles away from Florida Keys.

1) Which is the best way to rewrite sentence 1 to make it less awkward and to make its meaning clear?

   A) Most people are a combination of their inherited behaviors and internal and external frames.
   B) The truth is that most people are a combination of their met behaviors and internal and external frames.
   C) The truth is most people are a combination of their met behaviors and internal and external thoughts.
   D) Most people are a combination of their met programs and internal and external frames.
   E) The truth is most people are a combination of their inherited behaviors and internal and external frames.

2) Which is the best way to combine sentences 1 and 2?

   A) The truth is most people are a combination of their met programs and internal and external frames; however, if a child becomes too externally framed, they will be influenced by what the crowd is doing.
   B) The truth is most people are a combination of their met programs and internal and external frames and if a child becomes too externally framed, they will be influenced by what the crowd is doing.
   C) The truth is most people are a combination of their met programs and internal and external frames, in fact if a child becomes too externally framed, they will be influenced by what the crowd is doing.
   D) The truth is most people are a combination of their met programs and internal and external frames; although if a child becomes too externally framed, they will be influenced by what the crowd is doing.
   E) The truth is most people are a combination of their met programs and internal and external frames thus if a child becomes too externally framed they will be influenced by what the crowd is doing.

3) What is the best rewrite of sentence 2?

   A) However, if children become too externally framed, the crowd will influence what he/she is doing.
   B) However, if a child becomes too externally framed, he/she will be influenced by whatever the crowd is doing.
   C) However, if a child becomes too externally framed, the crowd will influence what they are doing.
   D) However, if children become too externally framed, he/she will be influenced by whatever the crowd is doing.
   E) However, if children become too externally framed, they will be influenced by whatever the crowd is doing.

4) What is the best rewrite of the underlined portion of sentence 3?

   A) thinking is that average people are barely paying their bills
   B) thinking is the average person in the crowd is barely paying his/her bills
   C) thinking is the average person in the crowd are barely paying their bills
   D) thinking is that the average person in the crowd is barely paying their bills
   E) thinking is that average people in the crowd are barely paying his/her bills

5) What is the best rewrite of the underlined portion of sentence 4?

   A) If Thomas Edison was an external thinker
   B) If Thomas Edison were an external thinker
   C) If Thomas Edison had been an external thinker
   D) If Thomas Edison could be an external thinker
   E) If Thomas Edison might have been an external thinker

VIII. PARAGRAPH STRUCTURE

Following is a paragraph from the draft of a student compsition with the sentences numbered for reference. Read the essay and then answer the questions that follow.

(1) Charles Henry is a successful general contractor who has built 47 communities in the southeast. (2) He remembers good times with his father building a clubhouse and a tree house in his back yard, where all the kids on the block used to play. (3) His father put him on the payroll when he was 11, and working on the weekends he earned enough money to pay for college. (4) However, after 3 years in college his father took ill, and he dropped out and helped him run the business. (5) He had so much enjoyment running the business he decided to earn his own general contractor license and is now Vice President of the company. (6) He says that even though many of his close friends are smarter and had better grades, most of them are struggling to find decent jobs.

1) Which of the following statements best describes the relationship of sentence 1 to the rest of the paragraph?

   A) It is the topic sentence; in other words, it establishes the organization of the paragraph as a whole.
   B) It is just the first sentence of several about the writer's background.
   C) It is not important to the paragraph as a whole.
   D) It could be left out without damaging the paragraph.
   E) It is an introductory sentence but not the topic sentence.

2) Which of the following statements best describes the relationship of sentence 6 to the rest of the paragraph?

   A) It is the topic sentence; in other words, it is the organizing idea of the paragraph.
   B) As the closing sentence, it completes the idea introduced in sentence 1.
   C) It is just another detail about the contractor's background.
   D) It is not essential to the meaning of the sentence.
   E) It is just extra information and doesn't play an important role in the paragraph.

3) Which of the following statements best describes the relationship of sentence 2 to the rest of the paragraph?

   A) It is the second part of a two-part topic sentence (sentences 1 and 2).
   B) It gives background detail that makes a bridge between the topic sentence (2) and the concluding sentence (6).
   C) It is just extra information and doesn't play an important role in the paragraph.
   D) Its purpose is to involve the reader emotionally.
   E) It begins a narrative sequence that leads from topic sentence to conclusion.

4) Which of the following statements best describes the relationship of sentences 3, 4, and 5 to the rest of the paragraph?

   A) They provide a narrative bridge between the topic sentence (1) and the concluding sentence (6).
   B) They merely provide background information.
   C) Together, they make up the topic sentence—the organizing idea of the paragraph.
   D) Their purpose is to involve the reader emotionally.
   E) They are interesting but not important to the meaning of the paragraph.

5) Which of the following statements best describes the relationship of sentence 5 to the rest of the paragraph?

   A) It is the conclusion.
   B) It introduces sentence 6, which is the conclusion.
   C) It restates the topic sentence.
   D) It is the topic sentence.
   E) It concludes the narrative sequence that leads to the conclusion.

IX. *WORD CHOICE AND IDIOM*

IN THE FOLLOWING GROUPS OF SENTENCES, CHOOSE THE SENTENCE THAT HAS NO ERRORS IN WORD CHOICE.

1)
    A) Consuelo felt that Tonio's family did not except her.
    B) Tonio's mother made a special effort to show Consuelo that she was accepted.
    C) Tonio excepted a flying job in Buenos Aires.
    D) Consuelo sold all of her homes accept the apartment in Paris.
    E) The time in New York City was enjoyable for Consuelo accept the last few weeks.

2)
    A) Tonio was sure that the differences in their culture would not effect their relationship.
    B) Consuelo knew that if she married Tonio, her income would be affected.
    C) The affects of the invasion of France were devastation of the first magnitude.
    D) The downturn in Tonio's career was the affect of his marriage to Consuelo.
    E) The time in the south of France effected Consuelo's health.

3)
    A) Tonio's mother tried to make peace between all five of the children.
    B) The owner of the airline had to choose between all the pilots.
    C) The benefits were parceled out among the pilots.
    D) Consuelo and Tonio had to choose between the three homes in New York City.
    E) Tonio could not make a choice between the three offers.

4)
    A) The lawyer was chosen because he was an uninterested party.
    B) Vivian had become disinterested in marrying Tonio.
    C) Judge Jones must remain disinterested in this case if he is to make an unbiased decision.
    D) Her former ardor had turned to disinterest.
    E) Consuelo was disinterested in moving to New York City.

5)
- A) Eventually, Tonio and Consuelo emigrated from Paris.
- B) Many Puerto Rican natives have emigrated to New York City in the last 50 years.
- C) Most U.S. citizens are the offspring of ancestors who immigrated to this country.
- D) People are emigrating from Mexico in large numbers.
- E) There were many French emigrations to America following the German invasion.

X. *VERB FORMS*

CHOOSE THE SENTENCE THAT DOES NOT HAVE AN ERROR IN VERB FORM.

1)
- A) The legs of the chair will be replace because they are wore.
- B) The dish had fell from the counter.
- C) I know that you have never drunk better orange juice.
- D) They believed that their son had died when the ship sunk.
- E) She announced that she was going to lay down and rest for awhile.

2)
- A) He had lead his country to victory.
- B) We have began using a new dry cleaner.
- C) The seam of the mattress had busted.
- D) He polished the furniture until it shined.
- E) The supervisor has spoken to the men about locking the door at night.

3)
- A) The books were lain on the table.
- B) We had shone her all the dresses in the store.
- C) My mother-in-law always complained that the dry cleaner had shrunk her clothes.
- D) I have not forgot the work I promised to do.
- E) This secretary had sat the folders down very carefully.

4)
- A) I had ran the same ad in the paper three times.
- B) Miss Clark has already shown us all the new products.
- C) The bedspread was already tore when I bought it.
- D) My granddaughter had
- E) He had showed me the steps in the process.

5)
- A) How many gallons of gas have we boughten this year?
- B) He has drove here from Phoenix three times.
- C) He has got three parking tickets.
- D) He laid down to rest after the grueling trip.
- E) He lay down to rest after the grueling trip.

Answer Key

I. PUNCTUATION
1. B
2. E
3. C
4. A
5. B

II. COMBINED SENTENCES
1. A
2. B
3. B
4. E
5. C

III. POSSESSIVES
1. E
2. A
3. D
4. B
5. B

IV. SUBORDINATION AND COORDINATION
1. B
2. D
3. B
4. C
5. B

V. IDENTIFYING SENTENCE ERRORS
1. D
2. C
3. D
4. E
5. C

VI. IMPROVING SENTENCES
1. D
2. A
3. D
4. B
5. A

VII. IMPROVING SENTENCES
1. A
2. A
3. E
4. A
5. C

VIII. PARAGRAPH STRUCTURE
1. A
2. B
3. E
4. A
5. E

IX. WORD CHOICE AND IDIOM
1. B
2. B
3. C
4. C
5. A

X. VERB FORMS
1. C
2. E
3. C
4. B
5. E

 Additional Sample Test Questions

Composition

1) When Columbus <u>sailed</u> from Spain in 1492 he <u>was</u> actually looking for a passage
                         A   B
   to India. When he reached America he <u>assumed</u> he had been successful and
                          C
   <u>had called</u> the native people Indians. <u>No error</u>.
       D   E

2) Mass <u>transit</u>, or public transportation, refers to transportation systems which <u>are</u>
           A   B
   available to the general public. <u>Including;</u> buses, trams, <u>subways and</u> other such
                                 C   D
   transportation systems. <u>No error</u>.
                               D

3) Fossil <u>fuels account</u> for about 88% <u>of</u> energy consumption in the United States.
                  A   B
   Of <u>that</u>, around 40% is oil, 20% is natural <u>gas</u>, and 20% is coal. <u>No error</u>.
       C   D   E

4) Cultural pluralism refers to situations <u>where</u> smaller cultural groups <u>are able</u> to
                                               A   B
   retain their cultural practices and still be accepted by the community. <u>Simply put</u>,
                                                                                          C
   cultural pluralism is when more than one culture <u>exists</u> peacefully in close
                                                                D
   proximity. <u>No error</u>.
                 E

5) The Krebs <u>cycle</u>, also called the citric acid cycle, is the process through <u>which</u> a
               A   B
   cell <u>converted</u> carbohydrates, <u>fats</u> and proteins into energy. <u>No error</u>.
           C   D   E

For questions 6-12 refer to the following essay:

(1) An oligopoly is a type of market which is characterized by the dominance of a few large companies. (2) Unlike a pure competition market, in which companies operate relatively independent of each other, the companies in an oligopoly are largely aware of one another's actions. (3) In addition to monitoring each other's actions they use strategy to determine their own moves and predict the moves of others.

(4) One type of game theory, and the most popular, is the Prisoner's Dilemma. (5) Imagine that two criminals are arrested for committing a crime. (6) They are split up and questioned separately. (7) If neither of them confess, it is likely that they will only go to jail for a somewhat short amount of time, maybe three years, due to lack of strong evidence. (8) They are both offered a deal. (9) If they confess they will get a shorter term of one year, while their partner goes to jail for a long time, ten years. (10) This makes the optimal strategy for both to confess, and only receive one year. (11) However not knowing what their partner will do or say under pressure leaves them with a tough decision.

6) Where would it make the most sense to add the following lines to the essay?

   Game theory is an important aspect of oligopolies. It focuses on the reactions of members of a group in different situations.

   A) After the last paragraph
   B) After the first paragraph
   C) After line 4
   D) At the very beginning
   E) It would not make sense to insert the lines in the essay

7) In context, which of the following is the best replacement for the word "strong" in sentence 7?

   A) Convincing
   B) Muscular
   C) Legitimate
   D) Powerful
   E) Defining

8) Which of the following is the best revision to line 10?

   A) This means it is smartest for them to only receive one year, and confess.
   B) This will make the optimal strategy to be for them each to confess, so that neither of them will go to jail for ten years, and they will each only receive one year.
   C) This means the optimal strategy is to only receive one year.
   D) This means that they both should confess, and only receive one year, because it is the optimal strategy.
   E) No change

9) Which of the following changes must be made to line 11?

   A) Insert a comma after "pressure"
   B) Eliminate the word "tough"
   C) Insert a comma after "However"
   D) Change "leaves" to "leafs"
   E) No change

10) In context, what is the best way to combine lines 5 and 6?

    A) Imagine that two criminals are arrested for committing a crime; they are split up and questioned separately.
    B) Imagine that two criminals are arrested for committing a crime, and they are split up and questioned separately.
    C) Imagine that two criminals are arrested for committing a crime but they are split up and questioned separately.
    D) Two criminals are split up and questioned separately after imagining that they are arrested for committing a crime.
    E) Imagine that two criminals, after they are split up and questioned separately, are arrested for committing a crime.

11) Where would it make the most sense to place a comma in line 3 (shown below)?

    In addition to monitoring each other's actions they use strategy to determine their own moves and predict the moves of others.

    A) After "addition"
    B) After "monitoring"
    C) After "own moves"
    D) After "actions"
    E) None of the above

12) Which of the following best describes the main idea of the essay?

   A) To discuss the difference between pure competition markets and oligopolies.
   B) To inform the reader of the existence of oligopolies in today's world.
   C) To convince the reader that the best strategy when confronted with a Prisoner's Dilemma situation is to confess immediately.
   D) To discuss what oligopolies are, and what game strategy is.
   E) None of the above

For questions 13-22 consider the following story:

   (1) It was six year old Tommy's first baseball game and he couldn't wait to wake up that morning. (2) He was out of bed at the crack of dawn and began finding himself something to eat for breakfast. (3) His team had spent a lot of time practising, over the past three week, and he was sure that they would win. (4) He went to the cereal cupboard and pulled out his favorite cereal. (5) Then he went to the fridge to get some milk. (6) It was then that he ran into a problem: he wasn't tall enough to reach the bowls. (7) He considered his quandary for a moment, then went around the counter and pulled over a stool. (8) He ate his breakfast, proudly.

   (9) His breakfast finished, Tommy returned to his room and began looking for his uniform. (10) He went through every drawer and pulled out every piece of clothing. (11) No uniform. (12) He searched under his bed, in his toy chest and in his closet. (13) Still, though, he could not find his uniform. (14) He ran down the hall and into the laundry room, dumping out every basket of clothing until it was found.

   (15) Tommy dressed quickly and gathered up his equipment. (16) Knowing that it would be time to leave soon, he started practicing his swing and imagined himself making a home run. (17) Then, his mother walked into his room. (18) "Yes," he thought excitedly, "it must be time to leave now". (19) But her words surprised him. (20) "What are you doing?" she exclaimed. (21) "It's two o'clock in the morning."

13) Which of the following would best replace the word "quandary" in line 7?

   A) Dilemma
   B) Breakfast
   C) Choices
   D) Position
   E) Surroundings

14) Which of the following is NOT a revision that should be made to line 3?

   A) Change "alot" to "a lot"
   B) Change "practising" to "practicing"
   C) Remove the commas
   D) Change "week" to "weeks"
   E) All of the above corrections should be made

15) Which of the following revisions to line 8 is correct?

   A) He ate his breakfast proudly.
   B) He, proudly, ate his breakfast.
   C) Proudly, he ate his breakfast.
   D) He ate his proudly breakfast.
   E) No change

16) In context, which line should be eliminated from the first paragraph?

   A) 2
   B) 3
   C) 4
   D) 7
   E) 8

17) What does "it" in line 14 refer to?

   A) His bat
   B) His baseball
   C) His uniform
   D) His shoes
   E) His jeans

18) What would be the best way to combine lines 10 and 11?

   A) He went through every drawer and pulled out every piece of clothing, but he still couldn't find his uniform.
   B) He pulled every piece of clothing, opened every drawer, and couldn't find his uniform.
   C) He went through every drawer, pulled out every piece of clothing, and no uniform.
   D) There was still no uniform after he went through every draw and pulled out every piece of clothing.
   E) None of the above

19) Which of the following revisions should be made to line 18?

   A) Remove the comma after "Yes"
   B) Move the period at the end from after the quotation mark to before the quotation mark
   C) Remove the comma after "excitedly"
   D) Capitalize "he"
   E) No change

20) In context, sentence 11 serves to

   A) Break up the monotony of the story through its abruptness.
   B) Bring the paragraph to a close.
   C) Show Tommy's calm reaction to the situation.
   D) Emphasize Tommy's shock because it is short and abrupt.
   E) None of the above

21) Lines 18-21 are primarily used to

   A) Display a larger meaning.
   B) Create a comic ending.
   C) Make Tommy look like a fool.
   D) Show his mother's annoyance.
   E) None of the above

22) Which of the following best describes the story?

   A) An excerpt from a historical novel.
   B) A passage from a scientific journal.
   C) A children's story.
   D) An excerpt from a literary work.
   E) None of the above

For questions 23-28 consider the following paragraph:

(1) Ethan Frome is a novel by Edith Wharton. (2) The book tells the story of Ethan Frome who had been injured in a "smash up," some years previously. (3) A flashback shows the story of Frome falling in love with his wife's cousin Mattie (who reciprocates his affections) who has come to care for her when she falls ill. (4) When his wife Zeena discovers this she intends to have Mattie sent away. (5) Frome and Mattie form a suicide pact, but instead the two are just permanently injured. (6) The book ends with Zeena caring for Frome and Mattie.

23) Which of the following corrections should be made to line 1?

   A) Italicize "Ethan Frome"
   B) Underline "Edith Wharton"
   C) Change the word "novel" to "work of fiction"
   D) Add a comma after novel
   E) Move it to the end of the paragraph

24) Which of the following would be the best substitute for the word "reciprocates" in line 3?

   A) Rejects
   B) Responds to
   C) Gives back
   D) Returns
   E) None of the above

25) Who does the word "her" refer to in line 3?

   A) Ethan
   B) Edith
   C) Zeena
   D) Mattie
   E) None of the above

26) Which of the following is a suitable revision of line 3?

   A) A flashback shows the story of Frome falling in love with his wife's cousin Mattie, who reciprocates his affections, who has come to care for her when she falls ill.
   B) A flashback shows the story of Frome and his wife's cousin Mattie falling in love after Mattie comes to care for her when she falls ill.
   C) A flashback shows the story of Frome falling in love with his wife's cousin, Mattie (who reciprocates his affections), who has come to care for her when she falls ill.
   D) A flashback shows the story of Frome's wife's cousin coming to care for his wife when she falls ill, and the two of them fall in love.
   E) Any of the above

27) Which of the following revisions must be made to line 2?

   A) Italicize "Ethan Frome"
   B) Remove the comma after "smash up"
   C) Change the word "previously" to "formerly"
   D) Change "had" to "has"
   E) No revisions needed

28) Which of the following best describes the main point of the paragraph?

   A) To describe the irony of the clichéd situation.
   B) To convince the reader that *Ethan Frome* is a literary work.
   C) To caution readers against forming suicide pacts.
   D) To summarize the events of the novel *Ethan Frome*.
   E) None of the above

For questions 28-32 consider the following paragraph:

(1) Strip cropping is a type of farming in which crops are planted in alternating strips, with one being the crop, and the other being some sort of grass or hay. (2) The strips are then lined at a right angle against wind, or slopes to maximize erosion prevention. (3) Contour cropping is a type of farming in which planting is along contours instead of up and down slopes. (4) This way excess water runs into crops farther down. (5) The two methods are most useful when practiced together in strip contour cropping. (6) This is when the crops are planted in alternating strips which run along the contour instead of up and down a slope. (7) This helps to decrease soil erosion and makes more effective use of rainfall.

29) Which of the following would best improve the quality of the paragraph as a whole?

   A) A stronger conclusion
   B) More information comparing the two types of farming
   C) An introduction to the paragraph
   D) More specific examples
   E) Checking to make sure all words are spelled correctly

30) Which of the following would be the best correction to make in line 3?

   A) Insert "specific" before the word "type"
   B) Insert "done" after the second occurrence of the word "is"
   C) Insert a comma after "farming"
   D) Change "up and down" to "on"
   E) Move the line to be after line 4

31) In context, line 7 serves to

   A) Better explain why contour cropping is useful.
   B) Tie up the paragraph and explain the benefits of strip contour cropping.
   C) Introduce the next topic.
   D) Offer a refutation of the preceding argument.
   E) None of the above

32) Which correction must be made to line 2?

   A) Change the word "maximize" to "minimize"
   B) Add a second comma after "slopes"
   C) Further explain what a right angle is
   D) Remove the comma after "wind"
   E) Move the line to the beginning of the paragraph

33) Which of the following describes the logic behind the organization of the paragraph?

   A) The methods are organized in order of how often they are used so that as the paragraph progresses the reader is more convinced to use the last method.
   B) The paragraph is organized in alphabetical order to make the paragraph seem like it has academic merit.
   C) The paragraph is ordered so that the first method is the least practical, the second method is the most practical and the third method is moderately practical.
   D) Strip and contour cropping are discussed first to give background information to help the reader understand strip contour cropping.
   E) There is no particular order to the paragraph.

For questions 34-45 refer to the following essay:

(1) The Civil War was one of the worst wars the United States has been involved in. (2) Although it was not necessarily the beginning of the war, the first battle was Fort Sumter. (3) What made it the Civil War so terrible was that every soldier killed was an American, meaning that the overall American deaths were greater than in many other wars combined. (4) The war started in 1861, but the tensions and problems that caused it were building for long before that.

(5) Slavery was one of the main issues behind the war; but it was not the direct cause. (6) What caused the first wave of states to secede was because of the election of Abraham Lincoln. (7) Not a single southern state had voted for him, yet he was to be the next president. (8) The war is considered to have begun with the secession of South Carolina, which was soon followed by the secession of Mississippi, Florida, Alabama, Georgia, Louisiana and Texas. (9) These states were later joined by others totaling 11 seceded states which called themselves the Confederate States of America.

(10) Fort Sumter was a military fort in South Carolina which the Confederacy demanded surrender. (11) Lincoln refused to surrender the fort and the Confederacy proceeded to bombard it. (12) Because relief did not arrive in time, they were forced to surrender and Lincoln began raising troops to take it again. (13) He got around the law requiring him to ask Congress for a declaration of war because he refused to acknowledge the Confederacy as a sovereign state, and instead viewed their secession as an insurrection. (14) So, the war began.

(15) The four year struggle between the two sections of the country changed the face the country. (16) Extensive damage had been done to areas where fighting occurred and even a new state was created (West Virginia). (17) However the war had positive aspects as well. (18) It kept the country together, and showed the states that the Federal government would not allow them disregard laws. (19) It also provided a way for the abolition of slavery.

34) Which of the following corrections should be made to line 3?

  A) Move it to the end of the essay
  B) Add a comma after the word "it"
  C) Put a question mark at the end instead of a period because it starts with an interrogative pronoun.
  D) Remove the word "it"
  E) None of the above

35) Which of the following line changes should be made to improve the flow of the essay?

   A) Move line 2 to be after line 9
   B) Move line 6 to be before line 5
   C) Move line 8 to be after line 6
   D) Move line 11 to after line 13
   E) Move line 15 the beginning of the essay

36) Which of the following corrections should be made to line 5?

   A) Change the semicolon to a colon
   B) Change the semicolon to a comma
   C) Add a comma after "but"
   D) Change "issues" to "issue"
   E) Remove the word "direct"

37) Which of the following would most contribute to the content of the essay as a whole?

   A) Talking less about how the war was started.
   B) Checking for correct spelling and punctuation usage throughout.
   C) Adding additional information about the major battles and the course of the war.
   D) Do not refer to the southern states as the Confederacy.
   E) No change needs to be made.

38) Which of the following corrections should be made to line 8?

   A) A semicolon should be added after "by" because it is the beginning of a list.
   B) A comma should be added after "Louisiana" because it is followed by "and."
   C) Only the name of the first state in the list needs to be capitalized.
   D) There should not be a comma following South Carolina because it is not followed by a conjunction.
   E) No changes must be made.

39) Which of the following is the best revision of line 13?

A) Because he viewed the Confederate States as insurrectionary, and not as sovereign states, Lincoln did not need to ask Congress for a declaration of war.
B) Lincoln was allowed to ignore any laws requiring him to go to Congress to ask for a formal declaration of war because he refused to acknowledge the fact that the Confederacy was a sovereign state. Instead he viewed their secession as an insurrection, which made it his responsibility to act.
C) Lincoln acted without asking for a declaration of war from Congress.
D) Lincoln was lucky that there was no law requiring him to get a formal declaration of war because most of the people did not agree that the south had no right to secede.
E) None of the revisions is better than the original text.

40) Who does "their" refer to in line 13?

A) The Confederacy
B) Lincoln
C) The relief
D) Fort Sumter
E) None of the above

41) What change should be made to the underlined portion of line 16 (shown below)?

Extensive damage had been done to areas where fighting <u>occurred and even a new state was created (West Virginia)</u>.

A) Move "even" to after "was"
B) Add a comma after "created"
C) Remove the parentheses around "West Virginia"
D) Add a comma after "occurred"
E) No change should be made

42) Which of the following would be the best correction to line 6?

A) Change "to secede" to "secession"
B) Remove "because of"
C) Add "recent" before "election"
D) Remove "What caused"
E) Remove "first wave of"

43) Which of the following revisions should be made to line 17?

   A) Change "However" to "But,"
   B) Remove the word "aspects"
   C) Capitalize "war"
   D) Add a comma after "However"
   E) None of the above

44) According to the passage

   A) The Civil War was directly caused by slavery.
   B) The Civil War was inexpensive.
   C) One of the main issues of the Civil War was slavery.
   D) There was no legitimate reason for the Civil War.
   E) None of the above

45) Which of the following most correctly describes the main idea of the essay?

   A) To discuss the major battles of the Civil War.
   B) To explain why slavery was not the only cause of the Civil War.
   C) To describe the events of Fort Sumter.
   D) To convince the reader that it was noble of Lincoln to abolish slavery.
   E) To discuss effects and causes of the Civil War.

46) Line 5 serves what purpose in the essay?

   A) To provide a resolution to the problem introduced in the first paragraph.
   B) To describe the main reason for the end of the Civil War.
   C) To indicate that although slavery was an underlying factor in the war, there were other factors which led to the immediate start of the war.
   D) To indicate that slavery was not an important focus of the war.
   E) None of the above

47) How is the title of the article indicated when citing a newspaper article?

   A) Italicized
   B) Underlined
   C) Quotation marks
   D) Bolded
   E) Parentheses

48) Which of the following is NOT included in the citation for a newspaper article?

   A) Author
   B) Pages
   C) Head of newspaper
   D) Name of newspaper
   E) Edition

49) Which of the following is NOT included in the citation for a book?

   A) Author
   B) Title of the book
   C) City of publication
   D) Day, month and year of publication
   E) Publisher

50) In MLA format, how should the title of the book be indicated?

   A) Underlined
   B) Bolded
   C) Quotation marks
   D) Circled
   E) Italicized

Answer Key

1) D
2) C
3) E
4) E
5) C
6) B
7) A
8) E
9) C
10) B
11) D
12) D
13) A
14) E
15) A
16) B
17) C
18) A
19) B
20) D
21) B
22) C
23) A
24) D
25) C
26) E
27) B
28) D
29) C
30) B
31) B
32) D
33) D
34) D
35) A
36) B
37) C
38) E
39) A
40) D
41) A
42) B
43) D
44) C
45) E
46) C
47) C
48) C
49) D
50) E

Test-Taking Strategies

Here are some test-taking strategies that are specific to this test and to other CLEP tests in general:
- Keep your eyes on the time. Pay attention to how much time you have left.
- Read the entire question and read all the answers. Many questions are not as hard to answer as they may seem. Sometimes, a difficult sounding question really only is asking you how to read an accompanying chart. Chart and graph questions are on most CLEP tests and should be an easy free point.
- If you don't know the answer immediately, the new computer-based testing lets you mark questions and come back to them later if you have time.
- Read the wording carefully. Some words can give you hints to the right answer. There are no exceptions to an answer when there are words in the question such as always, all or none. If one of the answer choices includes most or some of the right answers, but not all, then that is not the correct answer. Here is an example:

    The primary colors include all of the following:

    A) Red, Yellow, Blue, Green
    B) Red, Green, Yellow
    C) Red, Orange, Yellow
    D) Red, Yellow, Blue
    E) None of the above

    Although item A includes all the right answers, it also includes an incorrect answer, making it incorrect. If you didn't read it carefully, were in a hurry, or didn't know the material well, you might fall for this.
- Make a guess on a question that you do not know the answer to. There is no penalty for an incorrect answer. Eliminate the answer choices that you know are incorrect. For example, this will let your guess be a 1 in 3 chance instead.

What Your Score Means

Based on your score, you may, or may not, qualify for credit at your specific institution. At University of Phoenix, a score of 50 is passing for full credit. At Utah Valley University, the score is unpublished, the school will accept credit on a case-by-case basis. Another school, Brigham Young University (BYU) does not accept CLEP credit. To find out what score you need for credit, you need to get that information from your school's website or academic advisor.

You can score between 20 and 80 on any CLEP test. Some exams include percentile ranks. Each correct answer is worth one point. You lose no points for unanswered or incorrect questions.

Test Preparation

How much you need to study depends on your knowledge of a subject area. If you are interested in literature, took it in school, or enjoy reading then your studying and preparation for the literature or humanities test will not need to be as intensive as it would be for someone who is new to literature.

This book is much different than the regular CLEP study guides. This book actually teaches you the information that you need to know to pass the test. If you are particularly interested in an area, or feel like you want more information, do a quick search online. There is a lot you'll need to memorize. Almost everything in this book will be on the test. It is important to understand all major theories and concepts listed in the table of contents. It is also very important to know any bolded words.

Don't worry if you do not understand or know a lot about the area. If you study hard, you can complete and pass the test.

To prepare for the test, make a series of goals. Allot a certain amount of time to review the information you have already studied and to learn additional material. Take notes as you study-it will help you learn the material.

Legal Note

All rights reserved. This Study Guide, Book and Flashcards are protected under US Copyright Law. No part of this book or study guide or flashcards may be reproduced, distributed or stored in a retrieval system, or transmitted in any form or by any means, electronic, mechanical, photocopying, recording, or otherwise, without the prior written permission of the publisher Breely Crush Publishing, LLC. This manual is not supported by or affiliated with the College Board, creators of the CLEP test. CLEP is a registered trademark of the College Entrance Examination Board, which does not endorse this book.

FLASHCARDS

This section contains flashcards for you to use to further your understanding of the material and test yourself on important concepts, names or dates. Read the term or question then flip the page over to check the answer on the back. Keep in mind that this information may not be covered in the text of the study guide. Take your time to study the flashcards, you will need to know and understand these concepts to pass the test.

Syntax	Coordination
Subordination	Modifier
Comma Splice	Run-on Sentence
Sentence Fragment	Simple Sentence

How you connect ideas together	How words are put together
A descriptive phrase or word	How you make one idea subordinate to another idea
Two sentences put together without appropriate punctuation	When two complete sentences are tied together with a comma
One independent clause	An incomplete sentence

Compound Sentence	**Compound Complex Sentence**
Subject-Verb Agreement	**Pronoun-Antecedent Agreement**
Antecedents	**Idiom**
,	;

Two or more independent clauses with a dependent clause	Two or more independent clauses without a dependent clause
When the pronoun doesn't match its antecedents	When the subject and verb of a sentence don't go together
A phrase without a literal meaning	Going before, preceding
Semi-colon	Comma

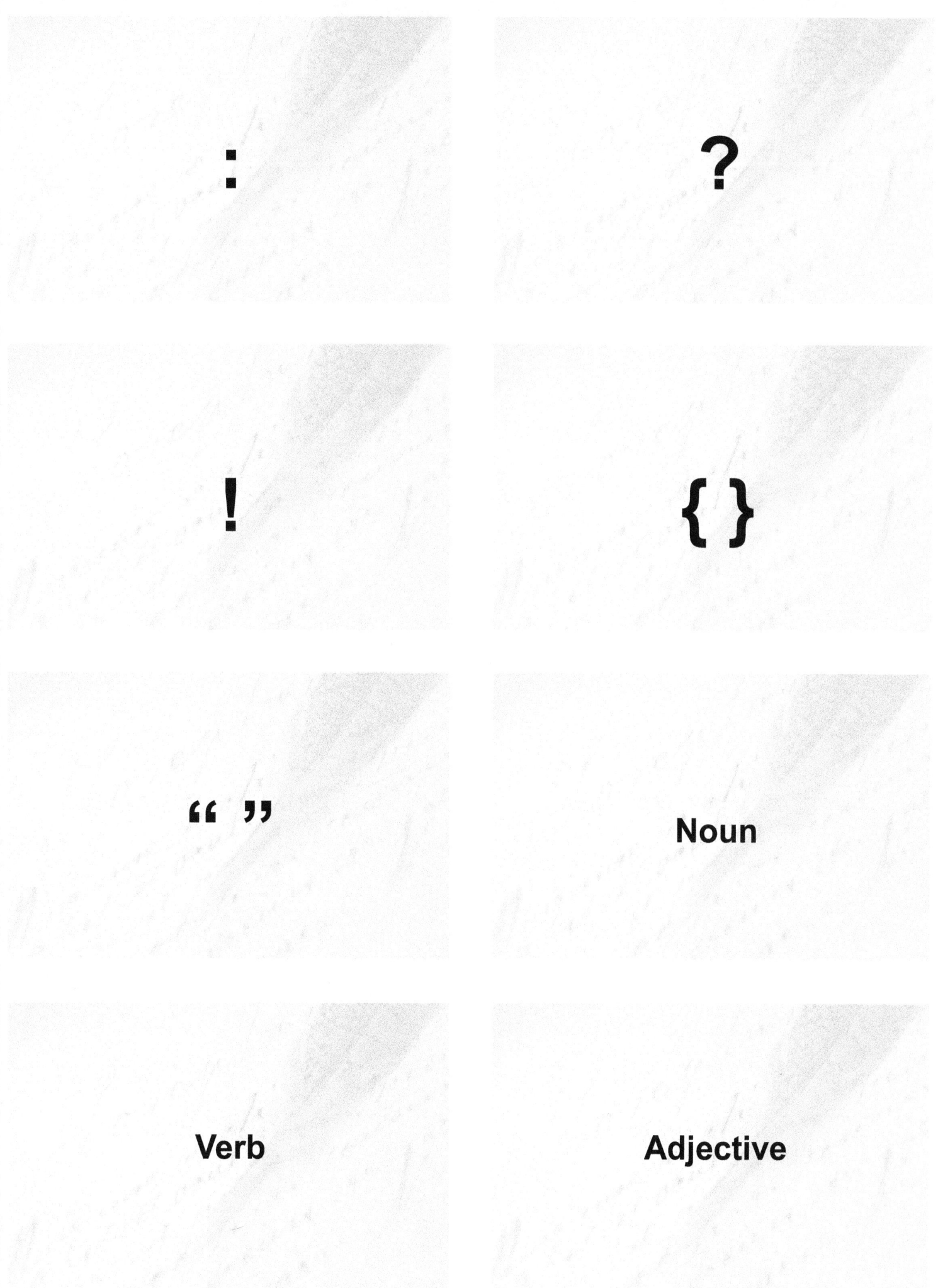

Question Mark	Colon
Ellipses	Exclamation Point
Person, place or thing	Quotation Marks
Modifies a noun	An action

Nominative Case

Objective Case

Possessive Case

Compound Personal Pronouns

Relative Pronouns

Interrogative Pronouns

Indefinite Pronouns

Agreement in Subject and Verb

Me, you, her, him, us, the	I, you, she, he, we, you, they
Myself, yourself, himself, herself, itself, ourselves, yourselves, themselves	My, mine, your, yours, his, her, hers, its, our, ours, their, theirs
Who, which, what	Who, that, which, what
The same in singular or plural form	All, any, both, each, either, everybody, none, one, several, some, someone

Diction Errors	**Idiom Errors**
Modifiers	**Verbs**
Base Form of Verbs	**Verb Form with -s**
Past Tense Verb	**Past Participle Verb**

Expressions that are not always clear from the meaning of the words (kick the bucket)	Incorrect word choices
Tell what the subject does or what is done to it	Describe words
He/she/it plays	I play
I have played	I played

Present Participle	Fragment
Comma Splice	Run-on Sentence
Topic Sentence	Restatement or Restriction
Illustration	Analysis

An incomplete sentence that is punctuated as if it were complete	I am playing
Two independent clauses that are not separated by a conjunction or proper punctuation	Two independent clauses containing a comma
The second sentence can restate or restrict what was written in the first sentence, making the subject more specific	The first sentence introducing the subject of a paragraph
Explain, interpret, and contextualize the illustrations that have been made	This section of the paragraph consists of the illustrations (evidence, data, facts, quotes, ect.) that support your topic

Conclusion	**Accept - define**
Except - define	**Affect (vb.) - define**
Effect - define	**All right - spelled correctly?**
Alright - spelled correctly?	**Among**

To receive	The final sentence (or two) might review what the paragraph has discussed, and/or reemphasize what is being suggested
To influence, to change	To exclude
Correct spelling	To accomplish (vb.); a result (n.)
When referring to more than two	Incorrect spelling

Between	**Continual**
Continous	**Disinterested**
Uninterested	**Emigrate**
Immigrate	**Eminent**

Recurring actions, repeated regularly and frequently	When referring to only two
Impartial	Occurring without interruption
One emigrates from a place	Not interested
Outstanding, distinguished	One immigrates to a place

Well	Respectfully
Respectively	Set
Sit	Unquestionable
Unquestioned	No exceptions

Courteously	An adverb when referring to how an action is performed
To put or to place	Each in the order given
Indisputable	To be seated
Always, every, all, only, never, none, not, must, necessary	Has not been questioned

Imminent	Ensure
Insure	Farther
Further	Fewer
Less	Good

To guarantee; to make safe	Threatening to happen soon
Describes distance	To provide insurance against loss
Used when nouns can be counted and made plural (fewer students)	Additionally; suggests quantity or degree
An adjective before a noun or after a linking verb (look good)	Used when nouns can't be counted or made plural (less homework)

| Antecedent | Denotation |

| Connotation | Transition |

| Pronoun | Conjunction |

| Interrogative pronoun | Fragment |

The literal meaning of a word.	A noun which is referred to using a pronoun.
A way to change to a new topic.	The implied meaning of a word (using context).
A word which is used to connect ideas phrases or sentence parts.	A word which takes the place of a noun (like it or that).
An incomplete sentence.	A pronoun used to start a sentence (who, what, which, whom and whose).

Participle	**5 x 5 essay**
Superscript	**Syntax**
Transition	**Flashback**
Clause	**Phrase**

A five paragraph essay which including an introduction and conclusion paragraph.	A noun which is used as an adjective.
Describes the way words are arranged in a sentence.	A letter or symbol printed above the text line.
When a story shifts to an earlier time.	A sentence or phrase which connects two paragraphs and adds to the coherence.
Part of a sentence which makes some sense but doesn't have a verb or subject.	Part of a sentence containing a subject and predicate.

NOTES

NOTES

NOTES

NOTES

NOTES

NOTES

NOTES

NOTES

NOTES

NOTES

NOTES

NOTES

NOTES

NOTES

NOTES

NOTES

NOTES

NOTES

NOTES

NOTES

www.ingramcontent.com/pod-product-compliance
Lightning Source LLC
Chambersburg PA
CBHW081832300426
44116CB00014B/2564